MW00889211

# Stop Spinning, Start Breathing

## A Codependency Workbook for Narcissist Abuse Recovery

*Zari Ballard*

Also by Zari Ballard:

**When Love Is a Lie**
*Narcissistic Partners & the*
*Pathological Relationship Agenda*

**Narcissist Free**
*A Survival Guide for the No-Contact Break-Up*

**When Evil Is a Pretty Face**
*Female Narcissists & the*
*Pathological Relationship Agenda*

ISBN-13: 978-1495253072
ISBN-10: 1495253074

# Dedication

*To my son  Sky:*

*I love you so much. You continue to be my inspiration for everything.*

# Table of CONTENTS

## *Note to Readers:*

In this book, when I refer to narcissists, sociopaths and psychopaths as being of the male gender, it is only for the sake of convenience and because I speak in great detail about my own relationship experience.

Certainly, narcissists and psychopaths do not exist only as boyfriends and husbands. They can, in fact, be male or female and come disguised as wives, girlfriends, mothers, fathers, sisters, brothers, sons, daughters, bosses, and co-workers. Whether the narcissist is male or female, all issues from the victim's perspective are equally important and just as distressing as any relationship described on these pages.

That being said, *Stop Spinning, Start Breathing* is dedicated to any **woman or man** in a committed relationship who is or has been subjected to emotional manipulation by someone with a narcissistic personality. Although it's a club to which none of us want to belong, as long as we're here, let's do what we all do best: *try to figure it all out.*

Only this time, we'll do it together...

With hope & sincerity,
Zari

## *What We Allow, Will Continue*

At that pivotal point when we realize that our partner is a narcissist or sociopath, we can also safely assume that we've been his/her enabler for a very long time. It's a crazy, addiction co-dependency that has *almost* as much to do with our allowing it as it does with the narcissist's manipulation. I say *almost* because I believe that credit should be given where credit is due – and the narcissist deserves most of the credit. Victims are manipulated into uncertainty to the point of second-guessing even the cold, hard facts. Our "love" life is continually played out on an unsteady high wire….that incredibly fine line between what we *know* is happening, what we *think* is happening, and what we hope *isn't* happening. So, when we do finally realize "what's up" and that – lo and behold – we were, for all intents and purposes, a willing participant, it's a hard pill to swallow. The good news, however, is that we can choose to accept it and vow to undo it, taking a giant step forward on the game board and moving us that much closer to mentally breaking free from this very toxic individual.

The truth of the matter is one that applies to just about any uncomfortable situation in life: **what we allow is what will continue**. If we allow the narcissist to disappear and reappear, to give us the deafening silent treatment over and over, and to press the proverbial relationship reset button whenever he feels like it, then he will continue to do so until the end of time. Keep in mind that to a narcissist, this kind of bullshit never gets old. He *loves it*.

1

It makes him feel gloriously alive and in control. If you allow it...hell, he's in narcissistic heaven. For you, there's nothing heavenly about it. It's an addiction scenario where you become the drug addict and the narcissist is both the drug dealer AND the drug itself. With every silence comes a debilitating sobriety and with each return he gets you higher than the time before. It's simply not a pretty picture.

I can talk about the perils of game participation because I was guilty of it myself for many, many years. If you've read my first book, *When Love Is a Lie*, you'd know that I spent almost thirteen long years loving a narcissistic abuser. What I allowed continued...and continued...and continued. To prove my point, let me offer two darkly comedic moments from my own enabler archives:

*One wee morning hour (around 4am), approximately two years and four silent treatments into the relationship, my ex and I were sitting in a studio (we were both musicians) playing guitar and having a grand old time. About eight hours earlier, he had finally called wanting to see me after six weeks of absolute silence. During those six weeks, I had been inconsolable, having no idea why he'd disappeared again (this being a time pre-"aha" moment, of course). I'd stopped eating, been unable to sleep, and written letter after letter trying to get him to respond but to no avail. Needless to say, relieved that he finally called, I happily accepted his invitation to get together. So, there we sat, singing, laughing, and me feeling very skinny, sleep-deprived, and as happy as can be when he suddenly put down his guitar, looked at me in loving amazement and pondered out loud, "Wow. Why do you love me? I don't even call you."*

Nice. My response, if I'm not mistaken, was to have sex with him right there on the studio floor. *Wow* is right. Even the narcissist was amazed at my enabling capabilities.

*Then there was the time, about six years later, that Wayne (yes, that's his real name), after cheating on me, getting caught, having no choice but to admit to it, and then trying everything - including smacking me on the head - to pull me out of my crying jag, finally realized he might have gone too far. Feigning remorse, he begged me to forgive him. I continued to sob, pleading "Why? Why? Why did you do it?" until the N, unable to pretend a second longer, threw up his hands in exasperation and yelled, "I don't know! I always figured I could do whatever I wanted and you'd still take me back!"*

My reaction to this burst of honesty escapes me (thank God) but let's just say that this particular incident occurred *after* the "a-ha" moment and about four years *before* we broke up…so, (sigh) we can all do the unfortunate math.

Over the years, there were countless times where I'd beg the questions "Why do you do it?" or "Why do you treat me this way?" to which he'd calmly reply, "Why do you let me?" I'd then counter with something brutally honest (but ineffectual) like "Because I'm an idiot" or something equally pathetic and implausible as "Because I keep hoping you'll change" or "Because I love you!"

Either way, what came to pass for me as a result was inevitable and, even now, gives me a knot in my stomach. I was a Narcissist's Enabler. And the fact that you're reading this probably means you've been a Narcissist's Enabler as well. In fact, I'm convinced that anyone who allows a narcissist to return after even *one* silent treatment is well on their way to becoming a Narcissist's Enabler.

The narcissist *uses* the silent treatment to not only gauge your level of codependency and/or enabling capability but also to gauge *his* level of control over you at any given time. This is why the silent treatment always appears to occur out the blue, catching us off-guard. Something that we do or say causes a warning bell to go off in the narcissist's twisted head indicating that we might not be as gung-ho for his program as he'd assumed. *Shit, what's going on here? Better give her the silent treatment so I can get the levels on this.*

**What we allow is what will continue**. And I understand this because I *allowed* for years and years. I was all apologies all the time without knowing what I was apologizing for. In the end, after nearly thirteen years, when I finally stopped allowing (and my levels kept coming back negative), the N left for good and he has never returned. That was a little over a year ago and not a word since. Obviously, the person(s) on the *other* receiving end of his narcissistic evil was - and still is (are) - being compliant. To whoever holds this coveted position, I say *good luck with that* and *better you than me*. But nothing about any of this is easy and the pain, while it's happening, is as painful as it gets.

This book is about feeling better....about getting back on the road to normal and away from the spinning. By "spinning", I mean the mindset of madness that prevents a narcissist's victim from ever getting to a place where feeling *better* – let alone feeling *normal* - seems even the slightest bit possible. Spinning is all about the *thinking*...the ruminating...the dwelling....the misappropriated concentration...the twisted focus...yes, it's all about *that*. The N encourages our spinning by giving us a long list of things to think and worry about, none of which are good and all of which are about him. If he's performed his narcissistic duties well he may not have to utter even a single word to get you to worry as hard as he'd like you to. Or he may choose to do the opposite, speaking the words "don't worry about a thing" with just the right inflection in his voice to keep you off-balance. Either way, you're smart and he knows it... so he's confident you'll get the message.

To those on the outside, the fact that we have to "recover" from *any* toxic partner may appear, at best, peculiar and, at worst, maybe even ludicrous. *Why would anyone have to recover? Why can't these whiners just shake themselves off and move on? Why all the damn suffering?* And, based on normal circumstances, I can even understand this way of thinking. But the truth, as you and I know, is that there is *nothing normal* about the circumstances a toxic, disordered narcissist will create in order to sabotage a relationship. There is no level to which he won't stoop, no rock under which he won't crawl, and no personal boundary over which he won't eagerly leap (like an evil Superman) in his quest to make another person insane. It's a mission so cleverly disguised at the outset that no one but the perpetrator himself is *ever* the wiser until it's far too late to back out comfortably. A person who has never experienced this type of relationship will simply never understand. So, that being said, if the narcissist's mask has finally slipped far enough for you to see underneath…if the a-ha moment has made itself horribly clear…if your emotions have been pushed to the absolute brink of destruction and your expectations of the relationship managed down to near nothingness, the next step, which can *only* go up, had better be on a path to recovery *or else.* Other than continuing to suffer in a manipulated reality, planning a recovery strategy for taking your life back is the only alternative.

Now…if only it could be that simple! To begin, let me ease you onto the right path via five important key points – or **recovery takeaways** – based upon the content of this book.

When our partner is a narcissist, by the time we figure it all out (and recognize our accountability), we've already accumulated an arsenal of emotional road blocks that eventually will stand in the way of our getting better. The biggest of these self-made deterrents is, of course, our enabling and the fact that we unwittingly become codependent on the very narcissistic drama that we hate. We actually become *attached to the suffering*. It's horribly unfair but it is what it is. Suffering over the narcissist inevitably becomes part of *who we are* (which, by the way, is *exactly* what the narcissist intended all along) and "spinning" is what we do to try to make sense of something that is entirely nonsensical.

Because our mental road blocks will never go away by themselves, it's imperative that we act aggressively about recovery. By this, I mean that we can start any time. No waiting until tomorrow or next week or after you've broken up or after you've given him one more chance to get it right. It means getting started *now* which leads me to:

*IMPORTANT TAKEAWAY #1*: *it doesn't have to be over between you and the narcissist, sociopath, or psychopath in order for you to begin working on recovery.*

Indeed, if we waited for the end, most - if not all - of us would never have a chance. Why? Because when you're involved with a narcissist, the possibility is very real that it could *never* end.

Why? Because, for a narcissist, watching you suffer never gets old, it just gets better. Furthermore, the narcissist *knows* that healing, for any victim, typically begins when a relationship ends so his entire purpose is to ensure that never happens. So, I emphatically encourage you to start your recovery *right now* while you're thinking about it or while this toxic individual is out of the room or while he's subjecting you to a silent treatment …and *even while he's in the middle of hoovering* to get you back. The sooner you start taking steps towards getting better, the sooner you'll start feeling the relief of detachment and the easier a break-up *of any kind* with the narcissist will be later on.

For just a second, put aside all notions of procrastination and assume that *today is the day* that you will finally put your foot down. If you're not ready for a confrontation or to go "no contact" – hey, that's perfectly okay! You can *still* put your foot down even if it's only in your mind. There's nothing wrong with keeping your recovery a secret from the N because, honestly, this isn't about him at all. It's about you! For the first time in a very long time, you are actually going to *stop spinning* and *start breathing* and it's really going to be okay.

As you move through the steps of this book, it's important to stay centered in reality – *your* reality. You already know what the truth of the matter is or you wouldn't be here hoping to get better and stronger. Your time as a super-sleuth investigator *is over*, my friend. There's nothing about the narcissist that you need to figure out or find out about *anymore*. Now going forward, whether you're in the relationship or out of it, it's all about figuring *you* out and where *your* head is at....which leads me to:

**IMPORTANT TAKEAWAY #2: the main reason that a narcissist, sociopath, or psychopath returns again and again is to make sure that you never move on from the pain he caused you.**

And while this isn't the *only* evil reason, it certainly is the Grand Daddy of them all. He doesn't return because he misses you or loves you or realizes the error of his ways – no, unfortunately, it's none of that. Narcissists, specifically, will return (or hoover) for the purpose of keeping victims in the queue alongside *all the others* for as long as possible, thus ensuring that back-up narcissistic supply is always available. You see, by pressing the relationship reset button, the narcissist **is allowed** to repeat the honeymoon phase over and over. The honeymoon phase is always fresh and new and narcissists *love, love, love* things that are fresh and new. And, hell, *we* love things that are fresh and new too but it's never long before the narcissist's fresh and new turns into *what the fuck* and we start - God forbid – questioning suspicious behaviors. To the narcissist, when our questioning and suspicions commence, it's like the picture tube on a TV going out in his brain. He literally can not compute the resistance.

*What did she just say? Where was I **when**? What? Is she speaking English? Who is she? Where'd the **other** girl go? Where the fuck is the channel changer?*

Then, with legs spinning in circles like a frigging cartoon, he's off to the races and the silence begins. He will literally punish us for ruining his good time (even though he would have left anyway *eventually*, of course!). Later, the inevitable incidents of narcissistic hoovering (via text, email, Facebook, or sporadic phone call) are just the N's way of "checking in" with his supply (that's you) to make sure you're still in grief-mode - *and if you're not, he'll be sure to change that.* Rarely lacking in confidence, the N knows all the buttons to push to make you feel and behave in very specific ways and the bottom line, to him, is that you'll be there when he gets back....that you *allow yourself* to suffer just enough to keep him interested but not enough to interfere with his good time. It's a twisted game of cat and mouse that is strangely addicting to the mouse even though the mouse never wins. Moreover, in *this* version, while the cat's away, the mouse *won't even play*. The mouse just waits. And the cat just does whatever he fucking pleases with all the *other* mice.

In order to get past the pain, we've *got* to look at the narcissist and see him for exactly what he is. Recovery from narcissist abuse, according to my thinking, is all about realizing that nothing about this person is real except for the fact that he wants to destroy you. He is a pretender...an emotional impersonator...an anomaly that spends every waking minute trying to compensate – in the worst possible way - for human qualities that he can never have. Love is boring. Peace and calm are worse. Happiness is unforgivable. An N only "puts up" with niceties because he has to – of *that* responsibility, he is very much aware. Why do you think he's so good at making us think he's the good guy? The N has learned that certain emotions produce certain results and so he uses "mimicking" to get him what he wants from people who can provide. This strategy, while certainly effective, only works around those who have yet to see beneath his mask and of *this,* he is also aware. In your relationship, for example, the N has likely figured out (or has a good idea) that part – if not all – of his gig *is up.* If this the case, you've probably noticed either a significant increase in the amount of narcissistic chaos being created (ridiculous fights, ludicrous accusations, nit-picking, trying to instill jealousy, gas-lighting) or an unusually long and torturous silence taking place (sudden disappearance, silent treatment, no calls, texts, nothing) or perhaps you're being subjected to a little bit of both (silence for a few days, then a mean text or voice mail, rinse and repeat). Bottom line is:

*IMPORTANT TAKEAWAY #3: if he knows you know, you may be on the verge of being (figuratively) erased. Let it happen.*

11

Seriously, if you think he might be erasing you (as he's done many times before), it's because you're close to finding out something he'd rather you not know right now. Nothing you do is going to stop it from happening. Take a breath and let it play out. In the meantime, while he's gone, silence appreciation (Part II – Exercise 2b) is going to save you from yourself.

So, now for the question that weighs most heavily on the mind when it comes to recovery: *How long is this going to take? How long until I stop thinking about the bastard?* Well, I browsed around the internet and it appears that nobody seems to know. Some "experts" say it's different for everybody, some say it takes about a year, others say it could take forever, and I'm giving my answer as:

**IMPORTANT TAKEAWAY #4**: *if you really make a commitment to some version of recovery, then you can plan on giving yourself one month for every year you've been in it to feel better.*

But you *must* become an active participant (as I'm sure you will). If you do nothing and continue to ruminate on The Relationship (which was imaginary, by the way), yes, it could possibly take forever. Or you could die. Either of those could come first and neither option is hopeful. OR you can commit to getting better one baby step at a time (just as you would with any other unhealthy addiction) and reap the instant reward – a *recovery deadline to look forward to.* After all, who wants to even *think* about recovering from *anything* without knowing when you'll see or feel the results? Not me, that's for sure.

Let's imagine that you've been living in narcissistic hell for five years and today you've committed yourself to doing the work for recovery. In that split second, just from making that decision, your focus will have shifted just enough so that feeling a whole lot better in about five months is a perfectly attainable goal. By this, I mean that you'll *feel* like doing things that normal people do – such as getting out of bed, going to work, meeting up with friends, watching a movie, listening to music, etc. – and you *won't* feel like losing it. You'll smile a little freer and laugh a little louder. And while this doesn't mean that you won't ever *think* about what happened or what he's doing (because you will), it does mean that your thoughts will be presented with much less fanfare. After all of the obsessing, waiting, and non-stop hoping, the relief you will feel will be noticeable. Finally, you won't be inconsolable.

***If you're the mouse, it's time to change the game.*** The relationship will never get better than the bad that it is – and nothing you can do or say can ever change that. We have to stop enabling. We have to stop allowing. If we do that, nothing – but *nothing* – can ever continue to hurt us. So, whether you've recently ended a relationship with a narcissist or sociopath or a narcissist/sociopath recently ended it with you or whether you're still in the middle of the mess and looking for help, my hope is that

13

the written exercises on the pages that follow will demystify the recovery process, enlighten and unburden your weary mind, and put the situation in its proper perspective. And that is my wish for you.

# *How to Use this Workbook*

This workbook is intended to help you "journal" about your relationship. My wish is that you will use it as a tool for putting the pieces of your broken heart back together.

If you glance through the book, you'll see that I've split the journaling process into three distinct sections: *Putting the Relationship in It's Proper Perspective* (Part I), *Working Through the Pain* (Part II), and *Moving Forward* (Part III). Each section contains a group of discussions and written exercises that serve as the actual lessons for that part of the recovery. By following this journaling process, victims who suffer the type of mental/emotional abuse dished out by narcissistic/sociopathic partners will finally get relief. It's a strategy that focuses, especially in the beginning, on managing the memories of our relationship that keep us stuck in the whole damn mess. Only by putting these memories in the proper perspective can we ever begin the purging process that eventually leads to recovery. I believe it can work because I've done it myself. And, in this workbook, we're going to journal together as a team – me and you.

Like my first book, *When Love Is a Lie*, this workbook was written from the heart and deliberately contains no medical jargon or psychological explanation for the behaviors of toxic people. For me personally, during those times when I really needed comfort and relief, clinical mumbo jumbo about narcissism did nothing for me. I'm fairly confident, even now, that it only takes *one book* out there explaining why these types of disordered personalities can never be fixed for us to *get* that part of the situation. But then what? Making the discovery – *finally* – that the person we love is a fake, while certainly giving us an "a-ha" moment, doesn't magically give us the ability to walk away or make the heartbreak any easier to handle. The problem, as I see it, lies in dealing with the *aftermath* – the emotional collateral damage - of what we have experienced or are *still* experiencing. And *that* became my starting point for this recovery workbook.

For me, the only relief I *ever* received came from sharing my experience with others who knew exactly what I was talking about and from writing all the ugliness down on paper. Albeit, most of my writing occurred in letters to the N (literally *hundreds* of letters during hundreds of silent treatments) but this only now serves to further confirm my theory. One anxious evening in 2011, after scribbling furiously for hours, I looked up after I was done and felt suddenly better. I realized, in a split second, that I'd *always* felt better after writing him a letter and, given the fact that his receiving my letters never brought about the change I'd hoped for anyway, maybe the *writing* of the letter was cathartic enough. After that night, I would write and write and then throw the letters out. The next year passed without the N receiving even a single written word from me although, in my sadness, I would write thousands more. And shortly thereafter, the relationship ended without fanfare. It's now been a year and I've yet to shed a tear on his behalf. Coincidence? I think not..

As we all know, writing things down is a powerful internal healer. Actually "seeing" your life in words is a healing process that is based in reality and nothing else. Rarely do we sugarcoat the passages of our diaries and journals and this is why these types of writings are so personal and profound. Sometimes we *need* to see our pain laid out in all its nakedness in order to understand it and to determine how best to release it or, perhaps, live with it. With this recovery workbook, although it is laid out in three sections, you are free to jump around to the exercises that feel the most comfortable and to which you can provide the most honest response. In my quest to make this a team effort, you will see where I have completed the exercise ahead of you in the grey shaded areas and you can follow my format for the "answers" or choose to do it any way that you please. If you don't feel ready or the thought of answering a certain question is overwhelming or irrelevant, then skip to the next. This is *your* recovery and *your* road to happiness or to "no contact" or to wherever it is that you want to go. I don't care *how* we recover from this time-wasting nonsense as long as we recover!

Two options relevant to actually completing the written work are as follows: 1) print out the pages of this book, staple it together, and work directly on those pages in the designated areas, or 2) buy a separate notebook to use exclusively for working on the sections as you read from your PC, tablet, or other device. Consider that the second option allows you ample writing room to complete the exercises and this is very important. However you choose to do the work, be comfortable and free with your thoughts and your words. Make this recovery your own and let nothing stop you. Make this recovery about saving the rest of your life.

# Introduction:
## *Clarifying the Moral Compass*

Loving a narcissistic partner or any other toxic individual with a borderline personality is one of the most thankless and mind-boggling jobs on earth. The relationship itself - with all its twists and turns – is far different than any other we might experience in our lifetime. Because a narcissist is seemingly born not only with the *ability* to deceive (as we all are) but an (eager) *willingness* and, it appears, a *necessity* to deceive as well, the depth of the betrayal cuts bone deep. Victims feel a level of despair that exceeds far beyond the typical drama-trauma of even the most dysfunctional relationship. So when people outside of the relationship – even those personally close to us - don't *get it*, it's simply because they aren't grasping the concept of what makes us – as "normal" people - different from *them* (the narcissists).

Here's how I look at it: we're *all* born with the ability to do bad things and to treat others badly but we're also born with a moral compass that, for the most part, prevents us from acting on those abilities. Although it certainly doesn't make us perfect, our moral compass *does* keep us human, allowing us to have loving relationships with the right people. In life, we feel emotionally connected to our moral compass and we expect everyone associate with to have at least some version of it. It all comes down to whether or not a person has the willingness to *cross that line*...not the one that separates good from bad but the one separating *good from evil*, thus adding yet *another* complex element to what outsiders "don't get" about having a narcissistic partner: that it represents a *whooooole other* level of line-crossing. The truth is that, if inclusion into a category for "evil" was based on the sum total of all the bad choices we've ever made (and especially those that affected other people), most of us wouldn't make the cut. A narcissist, on the other hand, as a human anomaly that *completely lacks* a moral compass and, thus, will not only cross that line a million times over but actually prefers to *live on the other side* of it, will happily qualify every time. No matter how and from what angle you try to spin it, the relationship is guaranteed to be a roller coaster ride from hell.

No matter how smoothly it starts, a relationship that involves one partner having a narcissistic personality will inevitably take a mind-numbing turn for the worst, leaving the victim partner in emotional shreds, trying to make sense as to why it all happened. The montage of disturbing events that starts to occur – one after the other after the other - feels, to the unsuspecting partner, like a series of emotional sucker punches, each one more painful than the one before. Typically, the nightmare starts long after we've grown attached to the narcissist's fake persona.....the person that the narcissist pretended to be....the person that we thought he was...the person that he is *incapable* of being.

Lacking a moral compass, a narcissist will stay in multiple

relationships, diligently working to keep partners unsure or unaware of the existence of the others, for as long as he can and even after it's clear that he needs to leave everyone alone. The fact that he causes pain to others is the fuel to his fire. Narcissists live their lives via the proxy of their partner's suffering and via the "rules and requirements" of the narcissist's pathological relationship agenda. My first book, *When Love Is a Lie,* is all about this agenda and how it very deliberately wrecks the victim partner. This workbook, on the other hand, is all about the recovery and how we can begin to mend the post traumatic stress of loving someone who seemingly exists or existed to ensure our emotional demise.

There's no way I could even begin to care about why a narcissist does what narcissists do or why a narcissist thinks and behaves like the devil's minion that he is. *I just don't give a rat's ass.* I make this point because if you, as a reader, are looking for clinical explanations, I don't want to waste a minute more of your precious time and I encourage you to seek out other information. For all others, consider the afore-mentioned my disclaimer and let's dig in! When it comes to this particular type of relationship, I believe that those of us who have – or still are – experiencing the nightmare will, at some point (if we haven't already) become perfectly qualified to write about it, talk about it, and advise others in similar situations. Mentally breaking free from what happened will *always* be a work in progress and we all need to stick together, to learn from each other, and to do our best to help prevent others from going down the same road. Above all else, I have complete faith that we can all survive.

So, without further ado, let's move forward.

# Part I:

# Putting the Relationship in its Proper Perspective

# Exercise 1a:
# Managing the Memories

I assume that if you're here reading and working in this workbook, you must certainly have an idea of how the narcissist behaves and manipulates. Consequently, most of the exercises created for this book are about understanding (not to be confused with *excusing*) those behaviors and putting the relationship, as a whole, in its proper perspective. It would be great if this were the type of relationship we could simply end without ever looking back but this is not the case. A narcissistic/sociopathic partner is like no other and to experience one makes "never looking back" nearly impossible. That being said, it's *how* you look back and how you choose to manage the memories that truly count when you're trying to recover and that's what this first exercise will be about.

When we leave or get discarded by a narcissistic partner or by someone we care about who has a narcissistic personality, we are often so crippled by the loss that we tend to forget just how awful a person he or she really is. We develop a type of *relationship amnesia* that I personally feel is more a symptom of narcissistic emotional abuse than it is, on our part, a conscious decision to forget. Much of this book, as you will see, is about *reminding* you of that awfulness lest you have a *permanent* lapse in memory and – God forbid – allow the monster back in your life. I know, first-hand, what the repercussions are of that particular memory lapse, having willfully allowed my exe to re-enter my life probably a thousand times in 13-years. My hope is that, by working through the exercises in this workbook, we can eliminate the probability or our ever doing it again!

The unavailable man/narcissist/sociopath – whatever you want to call him - is typically a very passive-aggressive individual with all the time in the world to wreck your life. A normal person simply doesn't have that kind of time on their hands to reserve for such mean-spirited nonsense. Being normal people, this is a good part of the reason that we let certain insane behaviors slide rather than call it out. It's hard for us to fathom that anyone – let alone a person that we love - would actually expend the time and energy that it appears that they expend in order to do the hurtful things that do. It just doesn't make sense...so we force ourselves to ignore it.

By creating chaos and confusion, the narcissist gets exactly what he wants – control – and it's all connected to the pathological relationship agenda that all narcissists and most toxic people live and "love" by. Unfortunately, those who are initially deceived by - and now happen to love these individuals - do not typically discover what's happening until it's far too late to break away easily. For this reason, I am telling you with great conviction that you can start your recovery from whatever point you happen to be in right now. This means that you can start your recovery even if you are still involved with this person. You can start today. It is never too early and it is certainly never too late.

Since a major slip-up during the Idolize phase could, potentially, thwart the plans of his agenda, a narcissist must spread his work out over a long period time. To a polished N, this is no problem because everything he does is a means to an end and waiting is just part of the process. When my online investigations finally lead me to answers, I was already seven years in and I thought I could *fix it.* I wanted my man to be the exception to the rule. Reading through story after story about narcissism in relationships, I was continually flabbergasted (and sickened) how everything I read mirrored my life. Even now, with everything I know about the dynamic of this disorder, I am *still* amazed at the how the behaviors and actions of both narcissist & victim become interchangeable worldwide. Not only do our narcissists behave in the same way, speak the same words, and tell the same lies, we – meaning you and I – react to all of it with the same level of lunacy! Our lives on this planet have become interchangeable. We're all riding the same roller coaster with the same monster. *How the fuck do we get off this ride and why the hell are we riding at all??* This book will give you the answers.

Far crazier than even the narcissist's hurtful nonsense is the tendency of victims everywhere to forget how awful the narcissist is once he's gone. I don't know what psychologists call it but I call it *relationship amnesia* and, to me, it's a very real phenomenon. Relationship amnesia is the mindset that keeps us from barricading the door and ignoring the hoover each time the narcissist reappears after a silence. It's the mindset shrouded in a separation anxiety so profound that it takes our breath away. It's a mindset that makes us *miss the narcissist* no matter what he's done to us. For all of the above reasons, it's so very important that we keep the reality of *what he is* and *what he does* in the forefront of our minds as we try to recover......as we regroup within ourselves and find our way back to some semblance of sanity.

For the following exercises, I will focus on the same – albeit expanded - list of narcissistic behaviors presented in *When Love Is a Lie*. Whereas my first book provided the list as a way to help the reader recognize the signs of narcissism, in this book it is being used as a way to help us remember *exactly* what it is that we're dealing with and trying to recover *from* ...and why our guy fits the bill. For this first exercise, I ask that you read through each of the behaviors on the list and then follow my resonating example from my own relationship with one of your own. Again, because I'm doing the work along with you, you'll always see my example in shaded grey italics preceding the bold sentences that indicate the reader's work area.

So, are you ready? Let's see how well we resonate with the following list of narcissistic behaviors and expectations:

### *Typical Relationship Behaviors of a Narcissist:*

1. The narcissist (N) demands that you tolerate and cater to his every need and always be available when it works for him. He, of

course, does not have to be available for you *ever*. If you dare to question his unavailability or show an emotional reaction towards a manipulative behavior, you will likely receive a "punishment" such as the Silent Treatment (a narcissistic favorite) or the proverbial cold shoulder (if you live together) as a reminder of who has control.

*I remember that I had to be available whenever he called - to the point where I would freak out if I missed his phone call. And he hated when I locked the front door and he couldn't just walk in whenever he wanted to so I made sure it was always unlocked. Although I was always angry at myself for giving in to his demands, I still did it because I didn't want the anxiety of the punishment. Now, he certainly never had to be there for me at all. In fact, he didn't even have to have a phone at times or even answer the door when I came by.*

**Did your N exhibit this particular narcissistic behavior? If so, provide at least two examples of this behavior and describe how this type of behavioral control made you feel during the relationship.**

_____

_____

_____

_____

_____

_____

_____

_____

_____

_____

_____

2. The N is aware that his passive-aggressive indifference (not calling, disappearing, etc.) hurts you. By acting aloof and secretive, the Narcissist is able to continually test the mental limits of your patience. The partner of a narcissist is always made to feel that something is slightly "off" and, thus, will feel compelled – and eventually obsessed – with finding answers to the unsettling experience of day to day life with a narcissist.

*He could literally ignore me for weeks at a time (with a silent treatment) over something completely ridiculous (e.g. me not being there to catch his calls). It never ceased to be a painful experience and I would become obsessed with getting him to break the silence, pounding on his door, leaving notes, voice mails. It was horrible [My book* **When Love Is a Lie** *details my behavior during a silent treatment and how I finally put an end to my own madness]. I also became obsessed with trying to figure it all out...internet searches...researching strange names and phone numbers that appeared to be connected to his other life. I was sure that being able to connect the dots would ease the unsettling feeling and give me the peace I was looking for – but it never did.*

How did/does your N make you feel day to day? Did/do you find yourself struggling to be at peace in your own mind? Do you find yourself pre-occupied with fact checking everything in hopes of finding answers to your own nagging questions? Keeping a victim on the edge of her seats 24/7 is a very common narcissistic tactic for whittling away at a person's self-confidence and security. Describe examples of this type of behavior in your relationship and pin point exactly how it made you feel day to day.

_____

_____

_____

_____

_____

_____

_____

_____

_____

_____

_____

_____

3. The N will jump at the chance to be physically abusive if you allow it because they always feel you deserve it. However, physical abuse being too obvious a slip of the narcissistic mask, the

N will typically rely on his venomous mouth as the most effective means of inflicting emotional abuse and controlling you.

*Although my ex-N found his sinister narcissistic strength in words and in silence (silent treatment), for the first eight years of the relationship, he would periodically be physically abusive....slapping me hard across the head and several times knocking me to the ground. Then, as I got mentally stronger in the relationship, I would fight back both verbally and physically and he started to slowly back off. One day, out of the blue, he announced matter-of-factly, "I'm not going to hit you ever again" and he never did – not one time. To me, however, the "decision" was so obviously more a strategic move to suit his own purpose in the relationship than a realization that what he was doing was wrong (of which there was no mention) that to hear him say it like that made me sick. When I look back on it, I don't feel that there was a difference between the physical and emotional abuse – meaning that I don't remember one being worse than the other. All of his behaviors – even those that were passive-aggressive – were so connected and so much a part of the overall relationship agenda and what he hoped to achieve out of any given encounter that the intensity of each event was the same. It wasn't until I started deliberately detaching from the emotional "hurt" that I felt any kind of relief.*

A good number of narcissists and sociopaths have either never been physically abusive to a partner or have not been physically abusive for any long length of time in the relationship. Even a narcissist knows that this type of behavior pushes the limits of what others outside of the relationship might be sympathetic to. Simply put, *emotional* abuse is much harder to prove from a victim's standpoint. My observation is that a narcissist will eventually *try it* at some point simply because he needs to know, for his own satisfaction, that we allowed him to *go there.* The truth however, is that the psyche of the narcissistic personality is primarily focused on causing *emotional* pain and this is why the relationship at times is so complex.

**Was or is your N a physical abuser or did/does he focus primarily on causing emotional destruction? Describe how this aspect of the relationship affected your own psyche and how you managed to justify it day to day. How did the level of the abuse affect the normal functions of you everyday life?**

_____

_____

_____

_____

_____

_____

_____

_____

_____

33

4. The N will cheat on you numerous times – of that you can be sure. If you catch him, he will dismiss your feelings, threaten to do it again to shut you up, or act as if you are making a big deal out of nothing. At the same time, he will accuse you of doing the very same thing. This is a distraction maneuver and one of the most hurtful ploys of a narcissist. *However,* because Ns are like children who give themselves away without knowing it, understand that whatever the N is accusing you of is exactly what he's up to at that moment in his life. **Turn his ploy into your advantage.**

*At one point, he was adamantly accusing me of cheating (which I wasn't) and then he just disappeared. When he showed back up two weeks later, he was full of apologies but never really told me where he had been. Then, he answered his cell phone thinking it was work and it was the OW demanding to know why he had left her. He had to talk to her right in front of me. I was devastated and cried non-stop for days. At first, he pretended to care but it wasn't long before he was screaming "Get over it!" From then on, when he accused me of cheating, I knew he was. When he accused me of lying, I knew he was. All I had to do was really listen to his words – his accusations – instead of screaming over him. He thought he was winning but the reality is that I always knew what he was up to because he told on himself.*

If your partner is a narcissist, infidelity is inevitable. If he hasn't already, he *will* cheat. This, of course, is the most crushing narcissistic behavior of all and the most debilitating for all victims emotionally. Make no mistake - a narcissist is as chronic a cheater as he is a liar. Prowling for new narcissistic supply provides a thrill that a narcissist simply can not and will not refuse should the opportunity arise. Again, it's all a part of the pathological relationship agenda – an agenda where the intent is to *make you worry and suffer* – and what better way than to sleep with other people? The saving grace, however, is that once we realize that the narcissist *can't help* but accuse us of doing *exactly* what he happens to be doing, simply listening to his words begins to save us a whole lot of anguished guesswork.

**Describe the cheating and infidelity that you either *think* happened or you *know for sure* happened in your relationship with a narcissistic partner. How *did* you know/find out and how did it make you feel?**

_____

_____

_____

_____

_____

_____

_____

_____

_____

5. Because a narcissist knows he is emotionally incapable of providing support, sympathy, or empathy, he will use his indifference to your life as a way to keep you unbalanced and confused as to his intentions.

*In 2001, soon after the narcissist and I got together, my son – who was 10 years old at the time – developed child-onset schizophrenia. So, during all of the narcissist's treatment of me and the relationship, I also had my son's suffering going on and our subsequent journey together to get a handle on the illness. This included hospital stays, numerous medications, doctors, the situation at school, and the general horror of the disease itself. The N, for the most part, would conveniently disappear during many of the most traumatic events, only resurfacing when things had calmed down. Looking back, I think I jumped through a lot of hoops to keep things separated so he wouldn't see the situation as a pain and use it as an excuse to leave me. I'm pretty ashamed of that now and I'm also very ashamed of him for not caring enough to support us. In 2006, I wrote and published an article online called "Schizophrenia from a Mom's Perspective – A Teenager Learns to Cope" and it became very popular. When I first wrote it, six years had passed since it happened and since we had become a couple. I showed the article to him one night and, although he was complimentary, he read it without any emotion whatsoever. I remember being quietly stunned that he acted completely detached to the horrific story as if it had happened to someone else, somewhere else, and that he had no connection whatsoever. It never affected him ever.*

Loving a narcissist is not only a thankless job, it's a lonely one as well. It's very, very common for the narcissistic partner to disappear at the most opportune times (i.e. when you need him the most) in order to avoid the *annoyance* of having to feign sympathy, empathy, and compassion in general. Situations where *he* is not the focus or won't benefit from the outcome in some way simply serve no purpose whatsoever in his life. This would include, of course, any event in *our* lives where having the support of the one that we love would be most helpful. In my case, despite the fact that we were together 13-years, there really weren't a whole lot of events in my life where I expected him to be present. But for those few that I did, he would literally kiss me good-by with the promise to be back shortly and *literally disappear* until he knew the crisis had passed – no matter how long it took! And, seriously, just having to type that last sentence....seeing it all spelled out for me...is further confirmation of the fact that, indeed, he was and is a fucking loser.

**How about you? Although a narcissist demands that we support him in every way, he will, in turn, choose to disappear at the very moment that we need him the most. I *know* you've experienced this type of abandonment in your relationship with the narcissist. Describe an example of this type of emotional abuse (and it *is* abuse in every sense of the word) and explain exactly how it made you feel.**

_____

_____

_____

_____

_____

_____

_____

_____

_____

6. Over time, a narcissist slowly ***manages down our expectations of the relationship*** by expending only the most minimal of efforts required in maintaining his role as a partner. The narcissist's rule is **"just enough, just in time"** to keep the farce moving forward and not a bit more. He will manage down our expectations so that we learn to expect – and accept – mere crumbs of attention. The N has no intention of filling anyone's expectation but his own.

*My N was an expert at managing down my expectations over time so that I would expect less and less from him in the relationship and he could get away with more. For example, every time he'd disappear, he'd stay away just a tad longer than the time before and then resurface as if he'd never been gone. After crying a river of tears, I'd take him back without really pushing the issue and risk and earlier departure. He knew this and played it for all it was worth. He also knew that I'd be home waiting for him to return because that was how he had managed it. Eventually, he could pretty much stay away as long as he wanted because he had all but trained me to wait. One time, towards the end, when he rightly thought he had pushed me a little too far, he forced out a few fake tears and said, "I always figured I could do anything I wanted and you'd still take me back." Oh my God, when I think of that now, it still makes me sick to my stomach.*

The fact that the N has *managed down our expectations* is not something we typically realize has happened until we stumble upon the phrase itself and discover exactly what it means. That said, when we do make the discovery, it usually triggers an "a-ha" moment relative to our *own* behaviors as well as to his. For most of us, as time passes in the relationship, we become well aware of the fact that we allow the narcissist to hoover back in without repercussions but we're not exactly sure why we do this. Nothing about this person's actions warrants any leniency yet we continue to give it, often without question. Our own behavior baffles and disappoints us. We think back to past relationships where we would *never* have allowed these things to happen and it becomes very confusing. Why, now, do we allow ourselves to be swept up "in the moment" by *mere crumbs* of affection? The answer is that our expectations of the relationship have been methodically, deliberately, and fairly brilliantly, managed down to the ground so that we robotically begin to give everything and, literally, *expect nothing* in return.

Think back to how your narcissist creatively performed the managing down of your expectations. If you can't recall specific events, simply recall those times when you allowed him back and then were shocked at how easily you gave in. *Those* were the times when his management tactics were working. Think long and hard about what he did and how he played the game to get his desired result – *you* - over and over and over. It's important that you realize just how deep the wounds of narcissistic abuse can go. There are *reasons* for your own incredulous behavior in the relationship – and it *isn't* your fault.

_____

_____

_____

_____

_____

_____

_____

_____

_____

_____

7. The N is very good, when he needs to be, at *mimicking* the appropriate emotions of normal people in order to achieve a

desired result or get something that he needs. In doing this, he is able to continually throw you off-guard by blowing hot and cold. This is how the narcissist snagged you to being with and how he is able to attract women to him whenever he needs narcissistic supply. This is also how he is able to make you think all is okay right before a Discard *so that his current vanishing act confuses and hurts you even more than the last one.*

*Wayne could always "trick" me into thinking we were having a good day by being funny, having great sex, being generally affectionate and complimentary... and then, at the last second, he would create some kind of weird chaos over something unimportant, absolutely crippling me on his way out the door. It was as if those prior precious moments had never happened – and, of course, for him, they hadn't. Unfortunately, I wanted so bad for things to work out that I fell for the same old hurtful trick every time.*

**Narcissists are very good at what they do and we, being normal humans with real feelings, are inclined to believe what we see and take it at face value. This is *normal* and we shouldn't beat ourselves up in retrospect over our own reaction to the betrayal or over the fact that we inadvertently "allowed" it to happen. Humans are innately inclined, at least at first and especially with people that they love, to *believe* a person's words. Narcissists, however, understand our inclination and will use it against us at every turn and when we**

**least expect it. Think back to the emotionally abusive tactics used by the narcissist in your life. How did this person follow through with his intentions to deceive you and why do *you* think you were so easily baited in believing?**

_____

_____

_____

_____

_____

_____

_____

_____

_____

_____

_____

_____

8. The N truly believes that *his presence alone* is clearly and abundantly sufficient to maintain the loyalty, trust, and affection that he expects from you in the relationship. Subsequently, the narcissist will postpone, withhold, or procrastinate on any of the continuing, normal efforts essential to maintaining any kind of meaningful relationship. He may withhold sex or fail to be interested in taking you out or he may be stingy with money and/or

his time. A stagnant relationship is perfectly okay as long as he is getting what he wants from you…as long as he is controlling your emotions and the situation itself. Again, this is another way the N manages down our expectations, allowing him to get away with more and more abuse.

*Wayne never went out of his way to do anything special with me and, if he did, it was always something that ended up being about him. He acted as if the fact that he showed up at all or whenever he pleased should have been enough for me and, unfortunately, for a long time it was. We never made plans to do things like normal couples and, if we did, it was he who would initiate the plan and then proceed – without fail – to disappear the night before as if the plans had never been made. I became so used to this behavior that I never really expected to go anyway even as the event drew near. And if I did seem hesitant about making plans, he'd just accuse me of living in the past. So, in thirteen years, although we went a few places together, he never took me anywhere – ever – on his own (like a date). We never went on vacation or out to dinner or anything like that. He simply couldn't make a plan and keep it and, therefore, I never had anything to look forward to the entire time we were together. I hate him.*

**A narcissist will always let us down – sometimes for the little things, sometimes for the big things, and *always* during the times that we need him the most. Narcissists are especially fond of ruining holidays, birthdays, and any type of**

celebratory event – particularly those that have nothing specifically to do with him. Unfortunately for us, although a narcissist never brings anything to the table, he fully expects his presence alone to be all the motivation we need in order to love him. Describe one or two times when you expected this person to be there for you and he wasn't. If/when confronted, what would be his typical response? If you have children together, describe a time where he let the children down and how you felt about this. Were your expectations managed down to the point that you didn't expect his support and he, therefore, was able to get away with these behaviors?

_____

_____

_____

_____

_____

_____

_____

_____

_____

_____

_____

_____

_____

_____

9. Because a narcissist has no capacity for a committed relationship, he is unable to fake an emotion of love for any extended period of time. Consequently, he will periodically subject you, his partner, to silent treatments, disappearing for long periods of time and returning whenever he's ready, expecting no repercussions for his behavior.

*The silent treatment was my ex-N's answer to everything. Every year for thirteen years straight, he would create a ridiculous fight sometime in October and then disappear without a trace until the holidays were over. During the first three years of the relationship, in addition to the holiday disappearances, he would subject me to a six-week silent treatment about every four months. Around the eighth or ninth year, in addition to the holiday disappearances, he switched to a two weeks on/two weeks off silent treatment rotation that lasted about six months (after which he'd stick around until, of course, October). During the final three years, he simply extended his October holiday break until around February and then returned to torment me until the next October. Just recently, I read an article that described narcissists as seasonal and then went on to explain how they typically spend summers here, winters there and vice versa. Every word of that article was spot-on. And, yes, a narcissist returns expecting little or no repercussion for his behavior.*

As any victim partner will tell you, the silent treatment is one of the most powerful weapons in a narcissist's arsenal of passive-aggressive punishments. Narcissists *love* using the silent treatment because it is the quickest way to manage down a partner's expectations and the most effective way to show who's in control.

To gather article ideas for my website, *TheNarcissisticPersonality.com*, I frequently study the search engine results to determine what frequent phrases and keywords are searched in Google by those looking for information on narcissism. With these results, I then create new and informative content – in essence, giving readers what they want. According to Google, the top search keywords (related to narcissism) almost *always* include the exact term "silent treatment" or related phrases. What does this *really* mean? Well, to me, it means that today's narcissists are more passive-aggressively sinister than ever before and that the narcissist's use of the silent treatment as a way to demean, demoralize, humiliate and punish others has reached epidemic proportions.

**I know how horribly sad, abandoned, and rejected my ex's constant use of the silent treatment made *me* feel. Did the narcissistic partner in your life subject you to silent treatments or, if you lived together, frequent cold shoulders? If so, for what "reasons" would he take this action and *how far* would he take it? Keep in mind that silent treatments and other similar punishments are always used to disguise or distract from what a narcissist is really up to - typically cheating or thinking of**

cheating. What do you feel now, in retrospect, might have been the *real* reasons for his silences? Did you have suspicions or did you feel that it was your fault? How did the abandonment affect your life overall and how long would he typically stay away? Did your N have a pattern?

_____

_____

_____

_____

_____

_____

_____

_____

_____

_____

_____

_____

_____

_____

_____

_____

_____

_____

10. A Narcissist is typically in total control of all communications in his relationships. This is necessary because, during silent treatments and any other times when he's up to no good, he will not want certain people to be able to communicate or contact him. Consequently, he'll often have no phone (that you know of) or he may have a secret phone or he may have more than one phone or, like my ex, he'll frequently change numbers so that you cannot contact or find him while he's with someone else or so someone else cannot contact or find him while he's with you. All communication is only when he wants it.

*I talk about the communication issue relative to narcissism quite a bit in* **When Love Is a Lie** *simply because the "cell phone game", without a doubt, became the biggest cause of my anxiety throughout the nearly thirteen years that Wayne and I were together. To quote from my own book, "If, at any given time, he was feeling particularly evil or planned to be with another source of narcissistic supply for longer than a week, he would opt to change his cell number, ramping up the insanity even further. He changed his cell number so many times during one three-year stretch that I became confused which number he did have when we were back together."*

*You see, changing cell numbers (and maybe even having different phones for different relationships) put him in total charge of all communications. Yes, my ex was the Manager of Communications in our relationship and he took his job very seriously. He had no problem at all cutting me off completely by disconnecting or changing his number. In doing this, he unequivocally placed a big, bold exclamation point after the word **silent treatment**. To me, it hurt to the point of making me physically sick but that was okay with him too – in fact, my pain was the intention. He never stopped with the number changing all the way to the end. So, in effect, we spoke only when he wanted us to....when things were working in his favor. When he was ready to make up or when he was done with the other relationship, he simply dialed me up from his new number and we took it from there. The cell phone game became yet another cruel and demeaning way to manage down my expectations....and, over all those years, he did it too many times to even count. And I let him. On that, shame on me.*

**How did the narcissist manage communications in your relationship? Was he readily available or mostly unavailable and did he appear to take control of the process? Did you feel anxiety over your ability/inability to contact him during certain times and was his cell phone, as it is for so many, a point of contention in kind is to a healthy relationship, how would you describe the level of communications between the two of you?**

_____

_____

_____

_____

_____

_____

_____

_____

_____

_____

_____

_____

11. Narcissists have no problem performing normal human obligations in the global arena of their lives (i.e. with other people and even strangers). This is why it appears that your partner gets along with – and is willing *to do things for* – everyone *except* you. If this issue became the cause of major fights in your relationship and a source of angst for you, there was good reason - *you were right*. The fact is that a narcissist will go out of his way to charm and impress strangers because every stranger could potentially one day become narcissistic supply. A constant supply will, in turn, bump up his confidence and self-esteem. With *you*, however, the person he has *already captured*, the N finds the expenditure of

civil treatment taxing to his mental reserve and not really necessary in the big picture.

*I knew that, outside of our relationship, the N was very concerned with keeping up appearances so, consequently, he made it a point to really get to know everyone that he worked with (and he had many, many jobs over 13 years). If a certain person gossiped about another, my ex would participate just to get on their good side. If someone complained, he'd participate as well and even offer a shoulder to cry on. Of course, he would always latch on to the girls in the office, sympathizing with this and that. It was constant, ridiculous, and embarrassing behavior that would, inevitably, get him into trouble at some point but he ignored my repeated warnings. Getting in good with his female coworkers was just too much to resist and he knew it made me jealous. Eventually, someone somewhere would hear he'd been talking shit and he'd have to move on. To a narcissist, future consequences warrant no immediate concern whatsoever.*

*So, when someone I am consulting with is suspicious of a narcissist's behaviors and particularly with his indifference toward only her, I always ask, "How does this he behave in the global arena?" It's a simple question but the answer will always be very telling. How does he act towards everybody else?*

**How did your partner treat you in comparison to how he treated others? If the difference was obvious, how did his behaviors make you feel and, if confronted, how did he**

respond to the allegations? Looking back, can you see now how your partner's behaviors in the global arena were directly related to his constant need to validate his self-esteem and self-image? Were others easily charmed?

12. Narcissists will never accept blame for anything that happens in a relationship. They will always blame the other person involved – you, his employers, his parents or siblings, co-workers, ex's, etc. In a narcissist's life story, his parents will always be abusive (and therefore responsible for his adult behavior) and all of his ex's (including you) will be bi-polar psychopaths.

*This is a given with narcissists. Nothing – but NOTHING – is ever their fault. Mine blamed everything bad that he ever did to me and to anyone on a bad childhood. He would go on and on about how abusive his mother had been – I mean, horrible things that I am not sure even ever happened. If he got fired, he ALWAYS blames himself or his boss or another worker. If he cheated, it was because of something I did. In the end, when it was clear I wasn't buying it anymore he would resort to saying, "Yup – just blame it on me – I'm the asshole!! You never do ANYTHING wrong". It certainly wasn't an apology and it had nothing to do with accountability. It had everything to do with hating and mocking me.*

**Narcissists are notorious for blaming others for *everything* negative that happens in their lives. Literally, it's not unusual for someone with a narcissistic personality to *never* accept blame and to be completely incapable of understanding how accusations could ever be made against them for anything. To blame a narcissist for anything is setting ourselves up for immediate retaliation so that we learn to never blame him**

again! Yes, "blame" makes a narcissist very, very angry. Describe your partner's reaction to blame or to any type of accusation – even those that are undeniably true. To keep the peace, did you find yourself accepting blame when it actually belonged to your partner? Did you find yourself apologizing for things you didn't even do? I did.

_____

_____

_____

_____

_____

_____

_____

_____

_____

_____

_____

_____

_____

_____

_____

_____

_____

_____

13. A narcissist, in a very passive-aggressive manner, will let his partner know that he expects to be the center of attention and that all his demands and requests must be met with enthusiasm. For those requests that, for whatever reason, you cannot fulfill, the N feels perfectly justified in asking it of someone else – and, specifically, of someone whom you might feel threatened by. This is why you may find yourself compelled to always be jumping through hoops to please him at every turn even if, in doing so, you complicate other areas of your life. In the back of your mind, you always feel threatened by some person somewhere in some weird, unexplainable way.

*For the first five years of the relationship, he would, whenever we "broke up" go out of his way to befriend certain girlfriends even though he spoke horribly about them to me at every turn. He particularly made a point to become friendly with the girls that I no longer spoke with due to reasons that had much to do with him! I would hear through the grapevine that he had "stopped by" to visit these women and it would make me insane. Other times, he would passive-aggressively dangle a female co-worker into the picture as a threat and to encourage jealousy or resentment. This, by the way, is called **triangulation** and it's a method narcissists are extremely fond of using to keep their partners in heightened states of anxiety at all times – whether your together or not. My way of trying to avoid the anxiety was to bend over backwards to fill all and any of his requests even when they were inconvenient or interfered with important areas of my life. If I* *dared to call him out on his behavior or on my suspicions, he'd proceed to gas-light, calling me ridiculous and delusional. This controlling, gas-lighting relationship behavior, also typical of narcissists, is used with the full intention of keeping the victim partner feeling off-balance, insecure, and unsure of their own interpretations of events.*

Did your partner go out of his way, using various forms of passive-aggressive triangulation to make you feel suspicious, jealous, or threatened by another person or persons? Was your partner prone to gas-lighting during certain situations, causing you to second-guess your intuition and suspicions even though *you knew* deep down that you were spot-on? Gas-lighting and triangulation – tactics intended to break down the confidence and self-esteem of a partner – will often be the cause of post traumatic stress in victim partners long after the narcissist has gone for good. If any of these methods, no matter how subtle, were part of your partner's arsenal, it's important to get it down on paper and work it through. In the space below, describe a few examples of those times where you remember being deliberately manipulated by your partner to feel a certain way.

_____

_____

_____

_____

_____

_____

_____

_____

_____

_____

_____

_____

_____

_____

_____

_____

_____

_____

If you answered each of the above questions honestly, you may be feeling a little uneasy right now and that's okay. In order to recover, it's important to paint a crystal clear portrait of the person that causes us pain. Although hard to look at, this picture confirms for us that the person we love is indeed a narcissist. Understand that you deserve to see it, your recovery demands it, and, believe me, when we're dealing with a narcissistic personality, there's no such thing as too much confirmation.

# Exercise 1b:
## Lies, Lies, Lies

I emphasized it in **When Love Is a Lie** and I'll emphasize it again now: *narcissists lie even when the truth is a better story.* Everything about the relationship is a fabrication....a big fat lie. The narcissist's habit of lying about everything - no matter how insignificant - is the core of our pain. It is the nucleus around which our pain revolves day after day after day. I truly believe that developing relationship amnesia is just one way that our brain protects us from having to obsess about the abuse even more than we already do. Our brain, in its attempt to make everything okay, chooses at a certain point to only remember the good stuff. But now....now that we're trying to recover... we have to focus on *all of it* including the lies. Not obsess, mind you, but *focus*. Focusing on the many lies told to us by the narcissistic abuser is how we put the relationship in its proper perspective. And this is what this section of the workbook is all about.

How strange that, almost as soon as the relationship is over, we can't, for the life of us, remember why the narcissist is so bad. All we can think about is the great sex or the last time he made us laugh or how long we've been "together" or how cute he is or whatever. Certainly, under normal circumstances, there wouldn't be a problem with thinking back on good times and cherishing certain parts of the relationship. But these are not normal circumstances. The fact is that none of what we remember as being good was ever real. Maybe those moments *felt* good to us while they were happening but true goodness is supposed to last longer than a few moments. For the narcissist, nothing – not a single part of it - was ever real because he felt nothing. I know that's hard to wrap your head around but it's the truth.

This exercise is about remembering the relationship as it truly was…the reality of it. When our heart hurts, we tend to bathe the sadness of the situation in a delusional light but "delusional" is not conducive to getting better. In recovery, we want to be very clear in our minds about what just happened - the abuse, manipulation, and, most importantly, the lack of reciprocated love. Unfortunately, we loved someone who clearly was not only unlovable but *unworthy* of love as well and we need to accept this fact. No more relationship amnesia or selective memory. No more sugarcoating the abuse and offering mental forgiveness where it's definitely not due.

Now, I know there will be a certain number of readers – just as there were with my first book - who will insist that I don't care about holding myself or those that I counsel accountable. My answer to that is that this point in recovery isn't about accountability anyway – at least for *this* moment. It's about betrayal and pain and your broken heart. It's about the butterflies in your stomach that never go away and the anxiety, the wondering, and the anger. Accountability is for another book at another time.

Right now, in order to heal, we must set aside the tears start putting the relationship in its proper perspective. Let's talk about some of the lies that we experience when we love a narcissist. I'll go first.

1. *Once, when he disappeared for two weeks...simply vanished...he finally hoovered with a text (as usual) saying he had flown back east to visit his sick father for two weeks and had just gotten back. LIE! I insisted that I saw his car around town but he insisted otherwise. LIE! Tickets, please. Nope, he said he'd thrown them out. LIE!*

2. *When he first came back around after being gone for three months and wanted to see me, he was going to come over but called to say his mother had had a stroke and was in the hospital and he couldn't make it. He even faked crying the entire call except he forgot to fake it right at the end, letting his voice completely go back to normal right as he hung up and I caught it. A call to every hospital in town confirmed what I knew. LIE!*

3. *When he'd moved of his apartment and swore up and down he was homeless and living in his truck. However, when he'd call, I could tell he was in someone's house and even heard voices in the background that he denied were there. It would take him a long to call me back if I left a message. Many other things led me to believe otherwise. LIE!*

Now it's your turn. Looking back, write a few paragraphs about your own experience. Describe a fictitious story, fabricated excuse, a lie by omission, or just *any* old lie told to you by the narcissist at any point during your relationship. The significance or size of the lie is unimportant because a lie is still a lie. Feel free to list as many as you can remember. Fill up the whole damn notebook if you like. This is a time to purge the demons no matter how painful the memory.

_____

_____

_____

_____

_____

_____

_____

_____

_____

_____

_____

_____

_____

_____

_____

_____

_____

_____

The narcissist's propensity for lying is at the heart of the emotional suffering that we endure throughout the relationship. For anyone to expect us to "just get over it" is not only ludicrous, it's completely unrealistic. Being lied to over and over and over by someone we love is the ultimate betrayal and breeds general mistrust all around. The lies of the narcissist spill over into other areas of our lives and disrupt the normal flow of things. It affects our children, families, and friendships. Without a doubt, this is the most damaging aspect of the relationship agenda and the more we purge...the more we *accept and release* the reality of the betrayal... the lighter our hearts will be.

# Exercise 1c:

## Navigating Cognitive Dissonance

By most definitions, cognitive dissonance is the psychological discomfort or torment a person feels when he or she holds conflicting beliefs about something simultaneously. In other words, when we struggle with cognitive dissonance, it means that we are torn between believing what we *want* to believe and accepting what we *know* to be the truth about someone or something. Under normal circumstances, cognitive dissonance can result in our making important decisions that ultimately work in our best interest or for the best interest of our family. When we're in love with a narcissist, this is rarely what happens.

Not always a bad thing, cognitive dissonance (CD) can help us to weigh both sides of a situation so that we can make the best choice based on the truth and on facts. It's not a bad thing, that is, until it keeps us from leaving a narcissistic partner or from maintaining "no contact" when we've made our escape. CD becomes a problem when it keeps us tethered to a codependency to hope that will never get us anywhere.

So, the hardest part about letting go of the N is our reluctance to accept what we already know to be true: *that nothing we experienced "as love" in the relationship was real.* The relationship was nothing more than a fabrication created by the narcissist to benefit the narcissist. All those things that we miss – the loving words, the gestures, the witty comments, the sex – were just the narcissist's way of future-faking us into believing the lie. Yes, they will even fake a future with us if that's what it takes to keep us as supply.

What we actually did experience were the clever workings of a con artist who knew exactly how to manipulate our heartstrings. Consequently, when it's over, we not only grieve the loss, we grieve in high definition color with all sounds and smells in tact. Our confusion about what we want to believe and what we know to be true – our cognitive dissonance – is like a bad trick the brain plays on the heart. And, yes, it is very sad.

The reality is that the narcissist hates all of us - you, me, and anyone who has a heart. He hates us because we are capable of loving. He has hated us from the very day we became his target. He hated us even while insisting that he loved us. He hated us even when the sex was unbelievably good. *Oh, but that couldn't be true, could it? Not the sex!* Yup, it's true. And, while we're on the subject, what *about* the sex? For me, *the sex* was everything. *But how could he not love me if the sex was so great? That's just impossible!*

For those of us where sex was the hook, even though the narcissist does a million bad things that scream hatred towards us, we cling to the sex and pretend that *that's* how he *really* feels. It makes no sense at all and we know it…but we do it anyway. And so it goes....our cognitive dissonance sends us to hell and back over and over. Struggling to accept that the entire relationship was a lie is difficult. Our heart wants to believe that the N must have loved us at *some* point even though we know damn well that *no one* who really loved us would have done what he did. This obviously not being our first romance rodeo, we nonetheless know deep down that something about this rodeo is different. Something is just a little *off* and we grapple with the confusion.

One thing that saved me from lingering in cognitive dissonance was my longstanding belief that things in life simply must be *logical* in order to be true. In other words, something said or done has to make sense before I believe it. It has to fit into the way the world works or I simply consider it a lie. Towards the end of my relationship, I used my belief in logic to fight back. *I'm sorry, Wayne, but that's just not logical and it couldn't have happened that way. You're lying. Try again.* With common sense at my side, I'd be very calm and this infuriated him. And since he had no intention of ever telling me the truth, he simply started mocking me about it. *Yeah, whatever. Logical, logical, logical. I'm sick of your "logical" bullshit!* Yup, he'd mock me all the way out the door and then, of course, he'd vanish.

You can't argue with logic. You just can't. And so it was hat I came to use logic to navigate my way up and out of the muddy waters of cognitive dissonance. And you, my friend, can do the same. In order to wake from the nightmare, we have to observe the process of recovery logically. Things that make sense are *good* for you and the narcissist, as we know, is completely nonsensical. We can't continue to postpone recovery based on our conflicting beliefs about the narcissist – particularly when it's clear that we *know* the truth. While a narcissist knows right from wrong, he simply doesn't care about it, and this is how he gets through life doing what he does. This isn't normal behavior and faith in a logical way of thinking keeps us from falling into that same trap.

So, escaping the confusion of cognitive dissonance isn't rocket science. It's as simply as choosing the most logical of your two conflicting beliefs as truth. **If it's not logical, it's a lie.** Our belief in only that which is logical ensures making proper decisions and it ensures our sanity. Again, the great thing about logic is that there's no argument to it. If a behavior, a story, or an excuse doesn't make sense – if it's *not logical* – then you don't have to believe it or feel intimidated into believing it. The truth is the truth – even the narcissist knows that.

This exercise is about recognizing your level of cognitive dissonance and understanding the choices that you have to make. I'll go first:

*Even though I know now it wasn't real, I still miss the way he'd hold my face in his hands when he kissed me.*

*Even though I know now he didn't mean it, I still liked it when he told me that he thought I was a really smart person.*

*Even though I know now it would have never happened, I still wish we could have grown old together like he always said he was sure would happen.*

*Even though I know now it was just a ploy, I still laugh when I think about how he would "affectionately" mimic some of my more dramatic mannerisms.*

*Even though I know he could care less about me, I can't help but hold on to the belief that surely he must think of me and my son many times in a day.*

*Even though he'd done it to me a thousand times and I have absolutely no reason to believe that the next time would be any different, I can't help but think that maybe he really has changed and finally he can stop with this bad behavior, realize what a good catch I am, and love me like I deserve to be loved.*

*Even though his stories and excuses for suspicious behaviors make no sense at all, he must be telling the truth because he says so.*

*Even though my gut feeling is telling me one thing, I must believe the opposite because, after all, he's my boyfriend.*

**In the section below, I've started a few sentences that you can finish in any way that you like. You'll notice that I start each sentence under the premise that you *already know* that the things that you miss about the N were fabricated. I've also provided some blank areas as well where you can develop similar sentences on your own based on your own experience.**

Again, writing things down is a great way to release the mental image of the lie itself and, so, with this exercise, we'll deliberately allow ourselves a few nostalgic moments. To navigate the waters of cognitive dissonance, we have to reconcile the fact that what we thought was real in the relationship was a lie. And when love is a lie, we simply have no choice but to make the right choice and it's a monumental step in starting over.

*Even though I know now it wasn't real, I still miss:*

_____

_____

_____

_____

_____

_____

_____

*Even though I know now his feelings weren't genuine, I still liked it when he'd say:*

_____

_____

_____

_____

_____

_____

_____

_____

_____

_____

_____

Now, create your own sentences representing the cognitive dissonance you feel about your relationships...the untruths that you can't let go of or the "wishes" for things that you know in your heart wouldn't have or will not ever happen. It is your understanding of the difference that will give you the strength to let go of the relationship. When we finally "get" this, then and only then can we begin to break our codependency to hope and, ultimately, our attachment to the narcissist.

_____

_____

_____

_____

_____

_____

_____

_____

_____

_____

_____

_____

_____

Somewhere at some point, we have to deprogram ourselves from the brainwashing of narcissism. We have to learn to make the right choices and to come to terms with our conflicting beliefs about the person that is hurting us. Once we do this, things start to calm down. Being confused about our feelings…knowing one thing to be true yet *feeling* something totally opposite…is exhausting and no way to live life. By creating situations that spawn the confusion, the narcissist whittles away our self-worth and we begin to doubt everything. This is how the narcissist creates our reality.

Keep your beliefs about this person in check at all times and you will start to see the forest for the trees. Things will go from dark to light and the narcissistic fog he has placed on your life will begin to lift. Being mindful of truth at all times is the only guaranteed way of working through the pain.

# Part II:

# Working Through the Pain

# Exercise 2a:
## Why So Much Pain?

To work through the pain, we first have to understand why there is *so* much of it and why *this* relationship is different than all the others. Again, this isn't our first rodeo…so what the fuck is going on? Why is this broken heart different from all the others? Why is it so damn difficult to just *get on* with it? Are we really as pathetic as we feel? Is a relationship break-up with a narcissist *that* different? Yup, you bet it is.

Oddly enough, most women and men who end up in a relationship predicament with a narcissistic partner are amazed (and disappointed) to find themselves behaving in ways that are completely out of character. It's as if the narcissist molds and shapes the persona of us that he meets (and targets) into lots of little weaker versions that, in the end, don't even resemble who we once were. We are transformed, seemingly in seconds, from confident, successful women and men into needy, whiny newborns…newborns that will eventually be abandoned not once, not twice, but *many* times over before the end comes. And in the end, we *feel* like rejected newborns because whether it ends because he never returns or because we've decided that enough is enough, we still have to start over going forward and I mean *start over*. Suddenly, it's as if the narcissist was the only person we ever loved or who ever loved us and we *know* this isn't true…yet we turn this fabricated memory into our catalyst for grieving. Lord Almighty, how did we get here?

First, all relationships end "sadly" for one reason or another. Sometimes the sadness is bittersweet which means that both parties love each other but have accepted the fact that, in the best interest of both, it all must end. Bittersweet sadness is what makes a tear-jerker movie a tear-jerker. Bittersweet sadness is what makes you leave the theatre rooting for *both* characters. So, no, breaking-up with the narcissist (a.k.a The Evil One) doesn't constitute bittersweet.

Other categories for break-up sadness might be anger sadness, cheating/infidelity sadness, realized-we're-better-as-friends sadness, grew-out-of-each-other sadness...or whatever. The point is that any of these sadness categories (yes, even the cheating/infidelity), while certainly justification for a break-up, has the potential to heal over time. Face it, there are simply some exes that don't deserve being hated forever – and this goes for you as well, in reverse. Time passes and we get over the hurt without even knowing it. Then, somewhere, someday, you'll see this person and realize that your first reaction isn't a jolt, or an urge to run, or bad butterflies in your stomach. You'll be able to give this person a hug, meet the new girlfriend or boyfriend, chat about the weather or even old times for a minute, and then be on your way feeling perfectly fine.

Now, understand that, with the narcissist, it will never be

any of the above – ever. And you *know* it. And *that* is the difference. *That* is why there is so much pain right now and that is why we feel the need to *recover* from the whole damn mess.

A break-up with a narcissist hurts because: 1) you loved him and you thought he loved you, 2) you loved him and found out he *never* loved you, 3) you loved him and found out he'd been with others the whole time, 4) you based your entire future on this false love (and he went along with it), 5) you forgave him for *everything* in hopes he'd see the error of his ways but that never happened, 6) you invested so much time – maybe *years* – for nothing and he offers no apology (in fact, he *blames* you for all of it, 7) his ability to erase you (and even the children, if you have any together) is still, to this day, hard to fathom, and 8) he's simply fucking evil …….*the list could go on and on.*

**It's important that you understand that *you deserve* to hurt. You are *not* being a baby, you are *not* being weak, and you are *not* losing your mind. Stop worrying about what others think because anybody who judges your pain obviously has *never experienced* this type of relationship *ever* so who cares what they think! And anybody who has experienced it will know *exactly* why you suffer and it's all okay. So, for this exercise, make a list of the elements of this break-up that make it different for you than all the others. Why do *you* think that the pain is so much harder to bear?**

_____

_____

_____

_____

_____

_____

_____

_____

_____

_____

_____

My point with this particular section is to let you know *that it's not your fault.* Toxic people are very good at what they do. When others don't understand why we have such a hard time letting go, it's because they don't understand the level of betrayal that's involved in these types of relationships. Much of the abuse is passive-aggressive and passive-aggressive abuse is all about control. It's hard to explain passive-aggressive manipulation because much of it is unspoken and takes place over a long period of time. In one of the reader reviews written for *When Love Is a Lie,* a woman wrote "wow, you've just described the relationship I've been in for 43 years". Forty-three years!! I almost fell off my chair. It made me want to cry, it really did. Can you imagine going through this bullshit for forty-three years? Either can I. But, obviously, the possibility is there.

*Stop Spinning, Start Breathing*

In the next exercise, I'm going to explain how to appreciate the silence of the narcissist's absence in the wake of a silent treatment or break-up. It took me years to realize the importance of using that time wisely and, when I did, it saved my life and my sanity. If any of you have read self-help books that talk about mindfulness and meditation, silence appreciation is very close to that. I promise you, it will do you a world of good and results come quickly.

# Exercise 2b:
## Silence Appreciation

As we talked about in the last section, the N/S/P creates so much havoc and chaos that we become immune to – and codependent upon - the constant din of the narcissistic nonsense. The noise that he creates, of course, is nothing but a distraction – a play of smoke & mirrors – to divert your attention away from what *he* knows *you* know about what he's really up to. Again, it's all in the strategy guide for the pathological relationship agenda and the narcissist follows it to a tee. He makes your world so frigging noisy that you can't possibly pay attention to *every* suspicious behavior (although you try!) or you'd make yourself crazier than you already are. The narcissist counts on this to happen and so he ramps up the volume with nonsense and bullshit and illogical lies until all you hear is the drone of the Charlie Brown "WUA WUA's" every time he opens his mouth. Then, while the noise and chaos is swirling all around you, he disappears or pulls a silent treatment because he's now free to go – at least temporarily – and, although you'll be suffering as intended – you will have been too distracted to really have connected with his malevolent scheme.

My initiation into the narcissistic world of silent treatments was a prime example of a narcissist's determination to get the pain just right. For Wayne, at least initially, it was a bumbling disaster because I honestly didn't get it. *A silent treatment? What's a silent treatment?* I swear to you...I didn't know what that was. I'd never experienced that with *anybody*, rarely even heard about it, and certainly never *expected* it. Consequently, the first two times that he tried to implement it, my unassuming reaction was to leave worried notes and voice mails showing nothing but genuine concern for his health and safety. I thought surely he must be *dead* to be gone so long. This, of course, completely thwarted his plans, forcing him to resort to Plan B which involved making up a quick story, returning quietly to the fold, and committing himself to getting better results the next time around. *Damn it, this isn't working. Doesn't the stupid bitch know I'm giving her the silent treatment?* Since the whole point of a silent treatment is to obviously be silent, I can only imagine his frustration when, by the second week, he realized that I had no clue he was trying to hurt me. At that point, his only option was to settle in, kick up some more chaos, and crank up the narcissistic noise.

A few months later, it was time for Silent Treatment Take 3. Determined to get it right, he cleverly added a little something extra to the mix for the very first time – he changed his cell number. At first, thinking his cell must have run out of minutes, I felt only mildly annoyed. It never even occurred to me that what was happening was deliberate. Even when days turned into a week and then two weeks, my only thought was that he was letting his phone *stay* off – and *that* hurt bad enough. For the first time, I felt sad enough to cry about the silence. *How could he do that? Why would he want to? I thought we were good together.* Then, as I waivered on the brink of depression, Wayne resurfaced, hoovering via text - only this time the son-of-a-bitch had a new number. The realization, to me, was unfathomable. *He changed his phone number? Changed it – as in got a new one? Who the fuck does that? Someone who hates me, that's who! So why is he standing here?* The silence was one thing *but this* blew me away. I couldn't get it out of my head. There are times that I *still* can't get it out of my head. As for Wayne, once he saw my reaction to his clever new trick, he knew he'd struck gold. With every silent treatment thereafter for the next thirteen years, he made the cell phone number change his permanent calling card.

Unfortunately, when the vanishing happens, the silence is painfully deafening. Yes, when the N leaves, he takes *all that noise* with him just for effect. Believe me, it's an intended discard residual meant to torment you in much the same way the noise itself did. Only worse. It is the silence that makes us panic – *OMG, I've got to get him back!* I was as guilty as all hell in this respect. As soon as the phone stopped ringing and all the commotion had halted, I literally was beside myself with anxiety. In the silence, my mind would be whirling a mile a minute, conjuring up all kinds of scenarios about the N and about what he might be doing and thinking and why he might be doing and thinking it.

In order to work through the pain of a discard, we must partake in a good bit of *silence appreciation*. You see, the silence, when it happens, in that split second becomes very representative of change and *we all know what we feel about change-* especially *that* kind. Just like the noise was all about *him*, the silence becomes all about him as well only this time it's worse because now you have no idea where's he's at. Basically, whatever we feel is a direct result of the deafening silence combined with overwhelming separation anxiety and, no matter how you look at that, this can only mean a broken heart.

So, how can we fix it and move forward? We do it by learning to appreciate the silence. Once you learn to do this, the rest takes care of itself. In *When Love Is a Lie*, I talk about a series of mental *shifts* that began to occur for me out of nowhere once I got a grip on the big picture and started letting go. This didn't happen until many, many years later and long after I'd realized the enormous role that the silent treatment was going to play in my relationship with the narcissist. Sick and tired of being sick and tired, one day I simply let him throw his usual idiotic rant without saying a single word in response. When he got up and walked out, I still said nothing. I let him go. I didn't cry. I didn't chase him. I didn't scream after him. In fact, I never got up from behind my desk. He was so busy lecturing the air that he never even noticed my peaceful expression but that was okay. After the front door slammed, I just waited in the quiet and, lo and behold, my reward for this mindful silence was an instant epiphany. Without the phone ringing (and me waiting to jump on it lest I – *God forbid* – miss his call), without feeling homebound in the nervous anticipation that he might stop by (and I wouldn't be there), without feeling that my life, from moment to moment, depended solely upon his next narcissistic move, I could finally *breath*. Wow…pretty amazing.

I decided right then and there that if Wayne considered himself disconnected from *me*, then anything that *I* wanted to do from that moment forward (or at least until he came back which I knew he would) was none of his fucking business. I was – albeit temporarily – free to do whatever I pleased. And, at that point, anything that I did would serve to be a beautiful distraction from the pain and that's exactly what I needed and now it's exactly what *you* need as you read this book and begin to get better.

Like everything else in life, silence appreciation following the discard begins with baby steps. That being the case, try to look at it this way: if you're still with the narcissist and believe he'll be back (like he always does), then take this wonderful time he gives you in between to do whatever you want. You know damn well that there is nothing you can do right now to keep him from doing whatever (or *whoever*) he's planning to do – so enjoy the time off! And if you feel that, this time, it really might be over or that you don't *want to want him back* anyway, then this is your time and *your time only* going forward to mend the old wounds. By taking total action and immersing yourself in silence appreciation, you *can* turn a silent treatment into a win-win situation!

*Even thought the silence is deafening, I've been here a thousand times before and I know dwelling on it is a waste of time.*

*Therefore, I am going to use the silence in a positive way by doing the following things:*

*1. Starting a journal that documents my feelings about the relationship. Every time I get a twinge of separation anxiety or an urge to contact him, I am going to write in the journal instead and I'm going to keep writing until the feeling goes away.*

*2. Go out with my girlfriends – especially the ones I've been desperately missing but kind of ignoring because the N never liked them. And I'm not going to talk about him at all while I'm out no matter who asks me. Not tonight.*

*3. Register for school or sign up for some classes. I'm going to do something for myself that makes me feel good about myself. And it has to be something scheduled so that I can put it on a calendar and see it ahead of me.*

*4. Plan something for me and the kids to do that will take up an entire weekend. And I'm going to turn off the cell phone while we're doing it.*

*5. Make a list of things I've been neglecting to do and see how many I can check off during the rest of this week. The list could include trivial household tasks or anything on this list. "Work on my recovery" is going to be at the top.*

*6. De-clutter my house. Get rid of every thing that I don't need by asking myself "Do I love it?" If the answer is no, I'm going to get rid of it. Clutter breeds emotional chaos and that's the last thing I need.*

*7. Dye my hair auburn red. That way, even if he sees me, he won't recognize me.*

*8. Go to bed early. When I stay up real late, it's usually because I'm worrying about him, what he's doing, waiting for him to call or text, writing him letters, investigating his bullshit, or driving around looking for him. Now I can go to bed without worrying about what he's up to. It's not my concern.*

*9. I'm going to designate a quiet place to sit for fifteen minutes every day. I am going to listen to the silence and soak in the non-noise. I am going to work up to two times a day, once in the morning and once at night.*

**Now it's your turn. Make a list of things you can do to appreciate the silence and also write, next to each item, the reason why you will be doing it. Make the list as long or as short as you need but think about each item. If you create a random list just to make a list, you'll never complete a single thing. Create a Silence Appreciation list and make it count.**

***Even thought the silence is deafening, I've been here a thousand times before and I know dwelling on it is a waste of time. Therefore, I am going to use the silence in a positive way by doing the following things:***

_____

_____

Keep a little notepad in your purse or pocket calendar for jotting down things you want or need to do as they come up. Get organized about your life. When our partner is a narcissist, the days, weeks, and months become an emotional blur and we get nothing done. If we do, it's only because we absolutely have to because, as you and I know, we'd much rather be sitting around filled with anxiety trying to predict the narcissist's next move – which, by the way, is *exactly* the intention of a narcissist's passive-aggressive nonsense.

The more that you practice silence appreciation, the better you'll get at remembering all those things that you wanted to do but never did because the narcissist was controlling your life. You'll find yourself saying "Oh yeah! I forgot about that! Cool, and now I can actually *do* it..." and it will feel good. And that's what you want...to feel good.

When I finally started appreciating the actual *silence* of the silent treatments/break-ups and using that time to do things that the narcissistic noise had kept me from doing, *that's* when things started changing for me. I wouldn't go so far as to say I started looking forward to the next silent treatment, but I will say that, after I started taking advantage of those silences to focus on *me*, I was less and less responsive to his return appearances.

You see, when a narcissist hoovers and returns, nothing changes. Ever. He just pushes the relationship reset button and picks up right where he left off with all his spoken and unspoken rules in place. He expects *you* to pick up right where *he* left off as well and that means following those rules as if he'd never been gone. Once you practice and get used to being free of his bullshit during the off-times, I promise you that you'll find yourself feeling more resentful than relieved each time he returns. I admit, for me, this feeling was unsettling at first because it meant I was standing up for myself even if he didn't know it. I had made a connection with the silence and it was very freeing. I felt like I had a secret and it felt good. I want you to have the connection as well but you have to allow yourself to do it. When you start taking advantage of the silence instead of succumbing to it in sadness or fighting it tooth and nail, your life will begin to change.

So, get started. Make every day that the narcissist is away Silence Appreciation Day. It's all about moving on, my friend.

# *Exercise 2c:*
# *About Those Boundaries*

What are your personal boundaries? Do you know? I'll bet you don't – at least not off the top of your head. I, for one, know that I'll have to really think about it for this exercise and it's not going to be easy. To me, personal boundaries are basically unspoken and represent something *about ourselves*...such as our deepest feelings or our most important belief systems...things based on our own integrity that we (should) protect from harm. We develop boundaries naturally and that's what makes them so personal. Even if we don't think about them – which, of course, becomes a problem - we still have them. I bet if you asked the narcissist what your boundaries are, he'd know! In fact, nobody in your life right now knows your boundaries *better.*

You see, over time, in *normal* relationships, partners typically figure out and learn to respect each others boundaries without having to be told and without having to ask. In *normal* relationships, we can even fight with our partner to the point of breaking up and *still* not be fearful that he or she will do or say something that 1) could get us fired, 2) could get us in trouble with the law, 3) could embarrass us in front of friends or family, 4) could put us in a financial bind or even financial ruin, or 5) tarnish our reputation in the community...and so forth. When your partner is a narcissist, there is *always* that fear and with good reason.

Narcissists, sociopaths, and psychopaths are natural boundary crossers and there isn't a boundary in this world that, to them, is untouchable or off-limits. Crossing boundaries is *what they do* and big or small, they like them all. Without having boundaries to cross *every day*, a narcissist will literally have nothing to do. Life will be "ho-hum" boring with no thrills whatsoever and he can't have that. To ensure this never happens, the narcissist taps into your boundaries early on by watching you and the way you live and work. Quite the impressive observer, the narcissist keeps a mental note of each and every fear, feeling, belief, and vulnerability he sees so that he can use one or more against you later in the most hurtful way possible. He has an entire mental list of things he "can hold over your head" if need be and *everything you've ever told him in confidence is on it.*

If we never make a conscious effort to take inventory of our own fears and vulnerabilities (See Part III, Exercise 3a), eventually we will find ourselves in trouble or, more than likely, trouble will find us. Boundaries protect things about us that are both fragile and strong. When we truly set boundaries, it means we that we understand – and respect - the lines of our own emotional and physical thresh hold and we will not allow *anybody* to cross. It means that we have inventoried our fears and vulnerabilities and now have committed ourselves to protecting them at all costs.

There's a host of self-serving reasons why manipulative, toxic people deliberately keep us so busy and hoping we'll forget our boundaries – albeit temporarily – is a big one. Always keep in mind that nothing a narcissist, sociopath, or psychopath does is random. When a narcissist crosses one of your personal boundaries, he is *intentionally* making the leap from bad to evil. Because my ex was so good at crossing boundaries I didn't even know that I had, I used to say he had an "emergency boundary bag" that he'd dig into only at opportune moments. For example, my finally calling him out on certain repeated behaviors that he'd been enjoying for some time with no repercussions would *certainly* warrant dipping into the boundary bag. *Oh yeah? Take away my fun? I'll show her! Eneey meeny miney mo, over the boundary here I go!"* The same goes for any time that the narcissist feels that his worlds may be colliding or that you're getting a little too close to finding something out. For that, he'll need to cause a fairly big distraction and there's no bigger distraction than crossing a personal boundary.

So, we really owe it to ourselves to know our boundaries. It's our only protection. Later in this book, we'll talk about deal-breakers which actually protect our boundaries. We need to draw those lines in the sand. The more we care about ourselves, the less chance the N has of breaking our heart during the next go-around.

For this exercise, we're going to uncover a few personal boundaries. I found that an easy way to do this is to think back to the times when the narcissist really crossed a line....times when he went above and beyond the norm of his evilness. In the spaces below my own examples, start writing about a few of these events. Those times where his behavior really struck an emotional chord are the times that he crossed a boundary that was likely very important to you.

*My ex had a penchant for threatening my work situation because he knew how much my job at the time meant to me. Therefore, one personal boundary concerned my job. To cross it, he would call me at work and harass me or threaten to call my boss.*

*He liked to threaten me with calls to CPS that I was neglectful (a common narcissistic tactic) even though he knew I was an excellent mother. Therefore, a huge boundary for me was my child. To cross it, he would threaten me with bogus calls to Child Protective Services.*

*He once called and harassed my mother over money that I never owed him because he knew how I felt about keeping my parents out of my personal business. Therefore, this boundary concerned my relationship with my parents whom I am very close to. To cross it, he called my mother and upset her. (Thankfully, she'll always be my mom no matter what and so she basically told him to fuck off)*

*He knew I took pride in my personal possessions so he would often destroy them, break them, or take them apart under the guise of "fixing" them and then leave them apart. Therefore, this boundary concerned a few possessions that I really cared about. To cross it, he once threw my guitar off the second story landing at his apartment complex. Several times he vandalized my car. Many times he would take one of my computers apart and leave it like that.*

**The above is just a short example but you get the idea. What were some of the personal boundaries the N ever crossed with you and how did he do it? How did it make you feel?**

_____

_____

_____

_____

_____

_____

_____

_____

_____

_____

_____

_____

_____

_____

_____

_____

_____

_____

_____

_____

_____

Putting these incidents down on paper will bring clarity to the insidious nature of boundary crossing. If the boundaries you've uncovered still matter to you, make a mental note. Allow whatever you've written to stick in your mind from this moment forward.

And don't ever let *anyone* do any of those things to you ever again.

## Exercise 2d:
## The Truth(s) About Closure

One of the biggest laments from anyone who has ever been discarded by a narcissist or sociopath is that *there wasn't any closure*. Oh my God, we'll say it over and over, whining and crying until either we believe it or everyone around us believes it: *"But I didn't get any closure! There's never any closure...I need closure!"*

So, now that we're working through all this pain, let's talk about this "closure" that we all want so bad from these unfeeling, uncaring, unlovable individuals. Since closure can mean different things to different people, then what *is* that unique, one-of-a-kind closure that, if we *had* it, would make this whole situation so much easier to bear?

I mean, since much of what all of us in narcissist recovery do is cry and weep and whine over the lack of closure, then we surely must know exactly what this closure is, right? Of course. And it shouldn't be anything we even have to *think* about, I would imagine, since we spend so much time grieving its absence.

Well, here's **Truth #1** (which is both the good news and also the problem) about this elusive "closure" character (and this goes for any type of ending to any type of relationship, by the way): ***there's no such thing.*** And I'll say it again. ***There's no such***

***thing***. I used to cry about it too every time my ex walked out the door and I didn't think he was coming back. I wrote letter after letter after letter demanding my fucking closure and I never did get it. It took me a long time to realize that it didn't exist and that the pain I felt over not getting it was really something else (more on *that* coming up).

What I realized, through much soul-searching, was that "closure" is a made-up word that people associate with a happy ending...a word that signifies or describes all those events that happen at the end of fairytales (thus, the fairytale ending)...the events that result in all the loose ends being tied up in neat little bows on pristine emotional packages. In real life, the term closure, by normal definition, simply doesn't – and can't – logically co-exist with an ending of any sort. Now, I'm not saying that, in life, there are no happy endings....but, damn it, they sure are far and few between. With that being true, how can terms like "happy ending" and "narcissist" even sit side-by-side in a sentence? They can't – so how in the hell can we even *think* (never mind cry) about this "closure" thing when it's very existence *ever* – and particularly in our type of relationship – is a complete impossibility?

Seriously, if we think about it logically, what "closure" could the N/S/P ever give us that would make a damn difference after all the crap he's put us through? And, since we can't even *define* the closure we want, how can an empty, shell-of-a-man narcissist even offer up anything close to what we think it is that we need to make it all better for ourselves? Moreover, I'm sure most of us got the finger on his way out the door or a hang-up or a nasty remark or maybe nothing at all – and that, I'm sorry to say, *was* our closure. The fact is that it's supposed to be *over* and anything that ends *when we don't want it to* is just not going to make us happy no matter how we try to spin it.

But I know and you know that, whether there is such a thing or not, closure and our lack of getting it hurts. So, for this exercise, we're going to pretend that closure does exist for a minute and that our tears for not getting it are justified. This being the case, let's write about it. Since not getting closure is one of the things that keep us from moving forward, my hope is that, by pushing the agony out of our ruminating brain and onto the paper, we can move past it. So, what is the closure that we didn't get? If we could have gotten it from the narcissist, what would it have been?

*You walked on me again and this time it's for good, I guess. I can tell you hate me because, again, you leave me with no closure. I don't feel good....I want to feel good like you do. You don't seem to have a problem with closure. As long as it's over so you can go do what you want to do, what do you care if I'm alone and miserable and missing you? I want you to say I'm sorry and that you know it was all your fault – every bit of it! Maybe if you at least said that, I wouldn't feel so bad. Maybe I'd feel some finality to the situation that would make it bearable. Of course, if you told me you were sorry and that it was all you, I'd probably cry even harder and beg you to stay so we could fix it...because you know I'm the most forgiving person you'll ever know in your whole life! You owe me closure and until I get it, my heart will never heal. And you do want my heart to heal, don't you? Oh yeah, you don't care about that. Then, for my closure, I just want bad, bad things to happen to you and I want you to think about ME while they're happening. Yeah, that's what I want, you sorry, selfish son-of-a-bitch.*

Now, it's your turn. Write from the heart about this closure issue. What is the "closure" that you didn't get? And how would it have made you feel better in your given situation? Imagine you could pluck the N from his current situation so that he's standing right in front of you. Now, demand your closure.

_____

_____

_____

_____

_____

_____

_____

_____

_____

_____

_____

_____

_____

_____

_____

_____

_____

_____

_____

_____

_____

_____

Now, as I mentioned earlier, it took me many, many years to realize that closure – by the definition that we all know and love – didn't actually exist **(Truth #1)**. I did, however, still have to account for the pain I was feeling.........which brings me to **Truth #2: what we really want is *revenge.***

If you think this sounds harsh (which I bet most of you do *not*), the next time your heart is breaking over the fact that the narcissist erased you from his life without giving you the closure that you want, replace the word "closure" with "revenge" in your mind and see which image paints a truer, more comforting picture.

Now, let's talk about *that.*

# Exercise 2e:
# The Revenge Factor

Thinking about getting revenge on these motherfuckers doesn't make us bad people and it doesn't make us just like *them*...it just makes us normal. Now, I'm sure, as a writer, I'm going to get a lot of flack (and bad reviews) for this particular chapter from readers who have never been in a relationship with a narcissist - but I don't care. It's worth the risk for me because I'm confident that all other readers will know *exactly* what I'm talking about. And besides, I, personally, couldn't write these types of books *honestly* without addressing what is a very *real* issue. Now, that being said, what I figured out, after realizing that "closure" didn't exist, is that we only cry about wanting "closure" because, in our moral, conscious-laden minds, wanting to perform atrocities on these animals seems...well...too narcissistic. What we really want is something else. The truth is...*fuck closure! We want revenge and we want it now!*

We might not be exactly sure what closure means and how it would make us feel even if we *did* get it... but *revenge*? That's an entirely different story! Most of us can easily imagine – even if it's fleeting - how vindicating a good dose of successful revenge on the narcissist would feel.

So, let's work with the revenge factor for a moment. Now, I'm being flippant about it, obviously, because I do want these exercises to be something other than another reason to cry about love being a lie. I want you to find, as I did, that there's always a bit of humor in the sadness (and the madness). Truthfully, humor, more often than not, helps us to measure - with precision accuracy - the *actual* level of importance of any given situation. Measuring the significance of *anything* through a veil of tears is rarely an accurate depiction of the true reality and I think we all know this to be true.

When the N discards us, the message he sends is that we are no more important than the dirt on his shoe. He erases us. He erases all of our history together. He erases the memories. He squashes us like a bug. And this hurts horribly....sometimes *unbearably*.....and we simply wouldn't be normal if we didn't imagine, in our shattered little minds, getting a bit of revenge....of making him hurt just like we hurt...of ruining his life and, more importantly, his next relationship...of making him regret the very day he was born! For an instant, when we think of this, we feel something close to *better* – and this matters, it truly does.

So, we're going to write about it for a minute or two. We're going to play it out in a statement to the narcissist and then let it go so that we can move on. Why? Because we are *not* narcissists and he *did not* succeed in destroying our soul (as he'd like to believe) and, therefore, we *can* imagine a scenario of revenge and then release it to the Universe. It's a part of the process of acceptance and letting go of the relationship without attachment. So, let's play it out in a statement to the N/P about all of the things you'd like to punish him for. Let's be honest to a fault and then let it go – and I'll go first:

*I'm angry that you left me and I really hate you right now. I really wish I could ruin everything for you. I want to make you suffer to the point that you actually feel the exact pain that I feel every time you walk away from this relationship as if it never meant a thing....for every time you walked out after creating a ridiculous fight just so you could disappear, for every time you decided to subject me to a Godawful silent treatment as punishment for some made-up crime, for every time you changed your phone number so that I couldn't find out about your other life or it couldn't find out about me, for every time you turned into a jerk right after we had great sex, for every time you compelled me to apologize when I didn't do anything wrong, for every time that I begged you to stay but you turned and left anyway, for the hundreds of promises you broke without blinking an eye, for all the times that I forgave you thinking that eventually it would matter but it never did, for all the hours that I wasted trying to investigate you and all of your lies, for all those hours I spent driving around in the middle of the night trying to find you but couldn't because you're so very good at what you do, for all those times you looked me in the eye and told me you loved me and that we were perfect for each other...for all those things, for all those times, I want you to hurt, to bleed, to feel sorry for throwing away our history together. I want you to feel something – anything – for me and for the life we were supposed to have together. But I know that you can't because you are what you are and, that, perhaps, is the true source of all my awful pain.*

Now, it's your turn to vent your peace about the revenge/closure factor in your relationship. You can 1) write a bit about your opinion relative to revenge (and feel free to do it from any angle), or 2) you can write *to the narcissist as if you were speaking directly to him,* explaining how you feel and what you think he deserves, or 3) you can do a little of both.

_____

_____

_____

_____

_____

_____

_____

_____

_____

_____

_____

_____

_____

_____

_____

_____

_____

_____

_____

_____

_____

It may be different for you but I found as I wrote my section that it wasn't so much about me wanting to list *the ways* that I wanted revenge as it was about me wanting to list *the reasons* why. I'm fairly certain that most who are reading this book will discover something close to that if you re-read what you wrote.

The truth is that we are, in most cases, not going to do a single thing to "get back" at the ex lest we become just like him. Unlike a narcissist, we *do* believe in and understand consequence and repercussion and how our negative actions can affect the people who we love and who love *us*. Thus, because of our normalness, our focus on the revenge factor will be naturally minimal and fleeting as it should be.

The truth is that we loved this person and *that* is why we hurt. We wanted him or her to feel our love and *reciprocate* with feeling. The fact that we know now, in understanding the vileness of narcissism, that he or she never loved us to begin with is the true cause of our pain. And, so, the best revenge we can get on these monsters is to feel better. With the pain and the hurt still fresh, I know that concept may be difficult to grasp. But the truth of the matter, my friends, is that a healed heart really is our best revenge. And besides, out of all the acts of revenge *that they deserve*, it's the only one that happens to be legal. So, we have no choice. We have to move forward.

# *Part III:*

## *Moving Forward*

# Exercise 3a:
## Facing Our Fears

One of the biggest reasons we stay in bad relationships is because we are afraid of other things. Fear is the number one crippler of emotions and, if allowed, it will paralyze us from living life. When the narcissist leaves or gives us the silent treatment, what happens? What happens when we think it might be over and that he *really means it* this time? How do we feel when we imagine that he *won't* be hoovering back in a week or a month or even a year from now? What's the first thing that we do?

We panic. We feel afraid. Okay, but *why and about what?* This is what we need to figure out – and fast! Do we fear being alone? Do we fear missing the abuse, the good times, the chaos? What is this *fear* that keeps us wrapped up in a cocoon of anxiety? The answer, believe it or not, has nearly nothing to do with the asshole narcissist. It has to do with our own flaws...flaws that *we get to ignore* the entire time that the narcissist is keeping us busy with ridiculous, hurtful, and crazy-making behaviors. Now, in the silence, we are forced to listen.

When the narcissist leaves or goes silent, typically we are left completely quiet and vulnerable with nothing but our own issues for company. I agree that it can be a very creepy feeling. For me, at the moment a discard or silent treatment began, it was as if someone reached into my head and flipped a switch, shutting off the background noise. I never realized just how fucking noisy the narcissist made my life until he'd officially make himself "gone" for awhile. There I'd sit with silence all around and knots in my stomach...no phones ringing, no texts beeping in, no nasty notes taped to my car window, no knocks on the front door or unannounced pop-ins...no *nothing*. Suddenly, in the snap of a finger, it all stops and the dysfunctional "noise" goes silent. The N, it seems, is fully in charge of turning it on, turning it off, and turning it *up* whenever he chooses and – make no mistake - it's a very intentional move each time. So, there I'd be, sitting in the silence, riddled with anxiety over *him* and scared to death of *my own painful weaknesses*.

This first exercise is about facing and trying to understand our own fears. Years and years ago, a child psychiatrist that I'd taken my son to see just a few times actually observed enough of *me* during those visits to make *this* statement to me one day: "*You have a fear of the mundane.*" At the time, I was puzzled and even mildly insulted at the observation but it sure as shit stuck in my head. In retrospect, I truly see that no truer observation about me has ever been made. He was spot-on! A fear of the mundane refers to a fear of anything ordinary or normal in life. Now, almost seventeen years later, I am certain that my fear of the mundane is what kept me addicted to the narcissist and his bullshit for over a decade. Like so many others, I became addicted to the very drama that I agonized over. After literally *hating* the drama while it's happening, the moment we think it might be gone for good, we panic. It's a Catch 22 that discourages our happiness. No one *wants* to believe that it's the chaos that we miss but the truth is *that it is*. In a twisted way, it becomes a part of who we are. We begin *identifying* with it. In fact, we identify with it to the point that it *becomes* us and we become *it*. We learn to live within the noise and actually find it comfortable. Then, when it's gone, the silence is deafening.

Because we've allowed ourselves to identify so strongly with it, the drama of the relationship has overshadowed everything. We get used to the narcissistic "noise" of the narcissist's existence in our lives and we miss it horribly when it's gone. In essence, we fear the silence of normalcy. We fear the calmness, the peacefulness of regular life. We fear the mundane.

Of course, there are other things that we could fear as well – rejection, abandonment, loneliness being just a few of those on what could be a very long list. And, of course, when we fear something, there has to be a reason *why* we fear it and to get to the bottom of that takes a little digging. Often, as we know, our childhood has much to do with how we behave as adults, how we interact with people, and why we do things that are detrimental to our well-being even though we are well aware of the choices we're making. Because I'm no psychologist or even slightly educated on the topic in any way, I can't begin to explain the psychological reasons for why we do what we do. This doesn't mean, however, that we can't begin the process of moving forward by at least trying to determine what our fears *are* so that we can release them even if we don't quite understand them.

For instance, there are a couple of family stories about me as a little girl that came to mind when I was thinking about writing this chapter. Up until now, except for the fact that, over the years, they've occasionally entertained the family, I never really gave these childhood anecdotes much thought. Now, though, I find these tales rather telling about how I've would later behave as an adult.

Much to the amusement of my entire family, I was, as a little girl, famous (or infamous perhaps!) for being very dramatic and highly emotional. Relatives dubbed me their "little Sarah Bernhardt", referring to a French actress of the early 1900's who was known for her over-the-top overacting abilities.

As my mom tells it, at the age of six or seven, I was quite a popular kid – so popular, in fact, that every day after school a rather large group of neighborhood girls would follow me home to play. This typically went well until dinner time rolled around and it came time for everyone to leave. Then, the drama would start. With mothers waiting out front and the announcement made that playtime was over, everything changed for me. As the story goes, I would run to the front door, throw my arms out dramatically to block the exit and literally beg for my friends not to have to leave. Exasperated, my mom would practically have to pry my fingers off the screen door so that my little friends could sneak past. She describes one little girl, who was new to the group and understandably mortified by the outburst, being consoled by another little girl who calmly remarked, "Oh don't worry. Zari does this every day. She'll be fine tomorrow." And every day, these little girls returned to play and every day I acted like they'd never return.

Other family anecdotes revolved around my tendency to burst into tears upon hearing just the opening notes of songs I apparently found to be very sad. Such songs included Andy William's "Moon River" and the opening theme song to the TV show "Flipper". From the very first opening notes, I turned into a sobbing ball of mush. My parents, who found this reaction to be most adorable, would often, at parties, prove the phenomenon to non-believers by calling me into the room and then dropping the needle onto the Andy Williams record. Much to the amusement of the party crowd and my parents, I would start wailing as if my heart had been broken into a thousand pieces. To this day, sad music has much the same effect on me.

So, what does this all mean? Maybe nothing except that I do know now that I've *always* been an emotional person...someone who cries easily about things that, much of the time, have absolutely nothing to do with me. I suppose you could say I am very empathetic, something that narcissists definitely are not. If you're reading this book, I'm sure you are the same way. Lovers of narcissists typically are. Did the narcissist know this about me...that I was empathetic? Sure he did. I knew my ex nearly a decade before he became my boyfriend. As a platonic friend, he was around for most of my marriage to my son's dad, the subsequent divorce, and then my next major relationship with a mutual friend. Did he know I was a *loyal* girlfriend and wife and an even better friend? Did he know how I felt about infidelity and about being lied to? Yup, he knew all of it.

Narcissists will target our vulnerabilities and "weaknesses" and use it against us at every turn. Even if you never knew the N before you hooked-up, it will take no time at all for him to figure you out. This is what they do. Having no emotions of his own, a narcissist finds the whole *concept* of emotions enormously fascinating and he will look for someone who has these characteristics. He's learned, through experience and practice, that manipulating, twisting, and even *mimicking* emotions can produce desired results. The narcissist is, after all, a great *pretender* and, thus, will try to mirror our goodness while at the same time taking it from us. Known for being a strong-willed person *outwardly*, I'm sure I confided the truth about my emotional self many times to my ex – someone I considered to be a close confidant - during those first ten years. Did he know that, for whatever reason (and I'll leave that to a psychologist to figure out some day), I had feared rejection and abandonment my whole life? Yes, I believe that he did. In essence, I was a perfect target for his pathological relationship agenda.

**Since I've already consumed much of this chapter with**

my own story, now, it's your turn. What do you feel are your fears and/or vulnerabilities? How did/do you handle the separation anxiety of a silent treatment? How do you feel the moment he leaves when you know he's not coming back? How do you deal with the anticipation? Can you think of any instances from your own childhood past that are telling of your behavior as an adult? Did your ex know your story?

_____

_____

_____

_____

_____

_____

_____

_____

_____

_____

_____

_____

_____

_____

_____

_____

_____

_____

A wise holistic doctor once told me, "If you face your fears, they will fall away of their own weight." Although facing our fears is never easy, he was absolutely right. Sometimes you just have to let the narcissist go and work through the residual damage. When we beg him to stay or beg him to come back, it's really more about our fear of feeling something we don't want to feel. It's more about our fear of facing our fears! I believe this is why we fall prey to toxic people and it's time to change. We've got to move forward to keep from falling back and taking inventory of ourselves is just another step in the process.

# Exercise 3b:
## Undeniable Truths vs. Obvious Reasons

In *When Love Is a Lie*, I dedicated a couple of chapters to what I refer to as my undeniable truths. By my own definition, an undeniable truth is a logical (there's that word again!) reason for detaching from and/or leaving the N that surpasses all other possible reasons. In other words, an undeniable truth is a reason for leaving for which there can be no argument (logical or otherwise) – hence, its undeniability. To develop those chapters, I knew from the start that in order for the truths/reasons that I had in mind to be undeniable, they'd have to be bigger and more meaningful than, say, the most *obvious* reason that we should leave the narcissist - the fact that he's *abusive* – because, as you and I know, that particular reason apparently isn't enough. So, in this exercise, as I did in *When Love Is a Lie,* I'm going to share my thought process in developing my logical truths to mentally set myself free and then using these logical truths to cut the ties once and for all and in this workbook, for this exercise, you're going to do the same.

When I began to mentally detach from my ex, it was about two years before his final walk-out. I already knew, at that point, that I'd allowed my boundaries to go all to hell and the realization was really forcing me to look at myself. Silent treatments grew longer and the time in-between grew shorter and shorter - over and over and over. At times, I felt like a neglected punching bag...a worn-out doormat…a nothing and a nobody. There was literally nothing he wouldn't do….no boundary that was off-limits…no time that he wouldn't find it appropriate to disappear. Then, out of the blue, he'd be back like he never left. As I'd cry, he'd tell me to stop dwelling on the past but how could I stop dwelling on the past when the past was only yesterday? It was gas lighting and manipulation and all the fuckery in-between…day after day after day.

Why do we stay in such an unloving relationship with someone who clearly has it out for us? Why is the fact that these human anomalies are *abusive* not enough to make us leave? *I needed to know why.* What on earth was it going to take? What reason would be good enough? *Uh, nope, not that one…could you throw me another…nope, not that one.*

For me, I knew that if I was going to stay, the least I could do for myself is detach (a.k.a. mentally break free) in preparation for an ending that I knew would come eventually. I had to come up with reasons for leaving that would be impossible to argue with…reasons that stood all on their own whether I liked them or not…reasons that made *so much sense* in the Universe that I would have no choice but to relinquish my grip on the sorrow of the relationship and let it all go.

Well, I did come up with some reasons and I call these reasons my undeniable truths. It was during that time that my perspective on day to day life with the N began to change…..my behaviors began to shift and the weight began to lift. Maybe I grew up or just woke up – I'm not sure. But it was all about finally deciding what is truly worthy of love in this lifetime – and it wasn't him. Now I would like you to try and make the same determination.

It's very possible that, when all is said and done, your undeniable truths will be very different from mine – and that's fine. *Just be sure you know what they are.* You may even call them something else and that's fine too. To me, an undeniable truth could be several things: 1) a quality a person *should* have, or 2) a quality they *are incapable* of having, or 3) a quality they should have but choose *not* to have, or 4) a quality I want or don't want in any person that I love and who loves me.

Once you decide what's really important to you in this life (and, face it, we *have to* decide sometime), to deliberately stay with someone who is incapable of having *any* of these qualities and who, at some point, has probably even *chosen not to* have them is unacceptable. These truths, when you finally decide what they are, will prove themselves to be undeniable and you will have no choice but to start moving in the right direction.

Nothing happens overnight so time is truly not an issue. This is why I say that you can begin right now, today, tonight, even if the N is in the next room. Once the Universe knows your intention, your life will begin to change for the better and you will notice the difference. You will begin to feel shifts in your behavior that will bring you great relief. Suddenly you won't obsess or cry at the drop of a hat or really be concerned that his call didn't come. You'll go to bed early or read a book or write a book or take a bubble bath or have a glass of wine or whatever you feel like doing. You'll suddenly be too tired to partake in a desperation ritual. Suddenly everything that you do and everything that you feel *won't be about the N*. It seemed strange to me at first because in many ways I had grown attached to my anxiety and it to me. Nonetheless, though, when my ex discarded me for the final time, I never shed a tear. The sadness was very different and I could tell immediately. I waited every day for the break down but it didn't come. I started to feel like hopeful about salvaging something wonderful out of the next half of my life after all. Maybe I *could* actually create memories for my son that didn't include his mother's broken heart.

Okay, with that said, my undeniable truths are about *cooperation and compromise* and, for lack of a way to explain it *better*, I'd like to include two brief excerpts from *When Love Is a Lie* to explain how I figured it out:

*"I came up with these truths by asking myself a couple of very important questions – questions I should have asked myself many, many years ago: What do I consider to be love worthy qualities in a person? In other words, what are the qualities – going forward - that I am going to consider, in fact, to be deal breakers.....the qualities that will determine who's company I keep*

122

*in the next chapter of my life? And, of course, we're talking about* **that** *kind of company at least for the moment.*

*The qualities, for me, that from now on will be my undeniable truths (my deal breakers to top all deal breakers) are a person's ability to* **cooperate and compromise** *so that everybody around him or her has a chance to be happy and this is why: I feel that "cooperation" is right up there next to love and money when it comes to what actually makes the world go 'round."* In that book, in order to paint a clearer picture of the type of cooperation I'm talking about, I ask readers to think of a huge, busy 4-way traffic light stop (every town has one) and to imagine themselves in one of those cars at that intersection. From that viewpoint, take a real good look at all the action going on around you. How does all that really work and, more amazingly, *why* does it all work? How does the person crossing at the crosswalk *really know* that the person in the car sitting at that light won't step on the gas? How do the cars in the turn lane *really know* that, even though they have the right of way, the first car in the oncoming lane won't gun it to try and beat the red light? How do the sounds of a fire truck or ambulance coming from *somewhere* cause all the cars in all the lanes - no matter what color the lights are, *all at once* and with no real confusion - to either sit still or move over to make way for the responders? Is it me or is that not frigging amazing? The truth is that we *have* no way of knowing what people around us – complete *strangers* - are going to do. Imagine if *nobody* did what they were supposed to do at that intersection. Imagine if everyone, walking or driving, just said *fuck it* and moved on into the intersection with no regard whatsoever for the people and cars around them? During every second of our lives, there is a possibility of that happening. *Why doesn't it?* Call me dramatic if you like, but that intersection is but a small piece of the big picture and we, for the most part, we take it all for granted. **Here's what makes it all work**: *cooperation and compromise.*

*"Cooperation and compromise are what marriages are made of ...and families and businesses and countries and governments. Some situations, without a doubt, work better than others and some might not even work at all...but the point is that, without cooperation and compromise, there isn't a chance in hell that we'd all survive another minute without killing ourselves or each other."*

What's really happening at that light – whether anyone knows it or not – is that **everybody has each other's back**. Somewhere along the line, a "normal" person learns to understand that, strangers or not, we have to place a certain amount of trust in strangers if we want to make it through our day. And we do it without even thinking. Sure, it doesn't work all of the time...but, for the most part, *it does*. That blows my mind.

So, when I can go about my day trusting a world full of strangers without giving it a second thought yet I have to worry minute to minute that the person I love, the person that I am committed to, will at any given moment, stab me in the back, lie to me, cheat on me, not be there to protect me or back me up…..*that's a bunch of bullshit and I can't do it anymore.*

**You've got to start looking at the big picture. What do you really want and how do you really want to feel in this life (and, by the way, it's the only life you've got)? Below, I give a quick synopsis of my decisions and then, in the space that follows, I want you to commit to a few of your own. Trying to get a handle on the things in life about which you now refuse to "settle" is the purpose for this workbook and the foundation for your recovery.**

1. *Going forward, I have decided that I won't put myself in another relationship with* a disordered personality that could care less about making those around him comfortable and happy. Narcissists, psychopaths, and sociopaths could care less about cooperation, compromise, or having *anybody's* back.

2. *Going forward, I've decided that I don't want to spend one more minute of my life – especially when I'm in a relationship - feeling* alone in times of crisis or feeling as if I can't call my significant other (whether we happen to be fighting or *not*) to rescue me from an uncomfortable situation. I can say with all confidence that I had my boyfriend's back countless times throughout the years and not once – I'll repeat that…not *once* – did he ever have mine.

3. *The qualities, for me, that from now on will be my undeniable truths (my deal breakers to top all deal breakers) are a* person's ability and willingness to cooperate and compromise in this life.

**Going forward, I have decided that I won't put myself in another relationship with:**

_____

_____

_____

_____

_____

_____

_____

_____

_____

**Going forward, I've decided that I won't spend one more minute of my life – especially when I'm in a relationship – feeling:**

_____

_____

_____

_____

_____

_____

_____

_____

Stop Spinning, Start Breathing

---

---

---

---

---

*The qualities, for me, that from now on will be my undeniable truths (my deal breakers to top all deal breakers) are:*

---

---

---

---

---

---

---

---

---

---

---

---

---

---

---

---

---

---

It's going to take a bit of practice to really see the world through an unobstructed set of glasses. Because you've been conditioned throughout your relationship to accept so much less than what you deserve, you've developed a complicated codependency that is based on expectations that never come. *This codependency deliberately keeps you separated from the present moment where the undeniable truths do the best work.* It keeps you looking backwards (to the past) or forwards (to an uncertain future). You're either worried about what happened yesterday or what could possibly happen tomorrow – and it's *never* good. And, make no mistake, this is exactly how the narcissist intends for you to feel...*co-dependently uncertain about everything.*

Let's see what we can do about that.

# Exercise 3c:
## Kicking the Codependency to Hope

Why do we develop such a twisted codependency to the narcissistic nonsense? Well, obviously there are a number of reasons – many of those that only a trained psychologist could explain. Since I'm nothing of the sort, I won't be defining *or* explaining codependency in a psychological "textbook" context but rather I'll explain what I know to be true based on my own experience, my keen observations, and my coming to terms with this whole damn thing.

Personally, I feel – and have come to believe – that the agonizing codependency that we develop when we love a narcissist is really more a *codependency to hope* than it is a codependency to anything else. By this, I mean that we become codependent to *hoping* the relationship will get better or that the narcissist can be fixed or that, realizing the error of his ways, he'll change on his own. All three possibilities, as we know now, are absolutely impossible but we never seem to stop hoping. During the process of developing this codependency, we inadvertently become the narcissist's enabler by allowing him to treat us in very disrespectful and demoralizing ways. It's horrible, it really is. And the entire time that it's happening to us, the narcissist is gleefully watching his plan take shape right before his very eyes.

The painfully slow evolution of this codependency to hope

is yet another intention from the narcissist's pathological relationship agenda. It begins with some very clever **passive-aggressive conditioning**...conditioning that is fully intended to make us feel desperate and insecure within the relationship. Since desperation and insecurity are two of the biggest catalysts for any type of codependency, it doesn't take a rocket scientist to make the connection. Starting with the idealization phase very early on, the narcissist whips us into shape using tactics deliberately passive-aggressive and deceptive in nature. In essence, he streamlines the path of our codependency to suit his own purpose. Granted, we allow it to happen but the bottom line is that *we are deceived from the get-go.* It doesn't matter how smart, how pretty, how educated, or how intuitive we believe ourselves to be. Deception is deception and narcissists deceive us into falling in love. This doesn't make it okay or erase our accountability for becoming codependent; it just makes it what it is. Narcissists are masters at what they do to "the unsuspecting" or they wouldn't be narcissists.

A victim's codependency to the narcissist's game of cat and mouse builds gradually just as the narcissist intends. The more gradual the build, the less likely we are to notice it's even happening until we are smack dab in the middle of the shit! At that point, we feel nearly powerless to pull out because there's always more to *do,* to *find out*, to *investigate*, and, above all else, more *bullshit* to put up with. The narcissist keeps us so deliberately *busy* shaping our own codependency that anything that we *need* to do that takes any amount of time at all simply doesn't get done. Again, the narcissist's behavior doesn't excuse our accountability...I'm just stating the facts. Instead of planning our escape, we spend our time hoping that *this time* it will be different...that *this time* we *can* love the narcissist out of his bad behavior and *this time* it will work. But we never can and it never will.

The victim of **narcissistic abuse** spends a good deal of her waking life in a relationship with a person who neglects her and will, in a moment's notice, abandon her. She is forever trying to figure out "the narcissist's secrets" - of which there are many – and this can take hour after consuming hour when desperation mounts. Keeping a codependency alive and strong in his victim partner is very much a requirement of the **narcissist's agenda and it *must* be fulfilled.** You might even say that he becomes addicted to this particular task. The victim, in much the same way, becomes addicted to the agenda as well but receives far less pleasure than the narcissist who literally thrives off of his partner's suffering.

**Certainly, to be codependent in a relationship** *without* the other partner having a personality disorder is hard enough. When narcissism is involved, it is inevitable that life will take a very dark turn. Codependents have a "high tolerance" pain thresh hold and will dutifully accept themselves as being damaged in order to "fix" another person. Typically neglectful of their own **personal boundaries,** codependents will willfully allow the manipulative partner to breach these boundaries over and over in the cruelest of ways. With a narcissistic partner, the victim will find themselves tolerating behavior they wouldn't have even *considered* tolerating prior to this relationship.

While a narcissist's claim to fame will *always* be his penchant for crossing the most private, pain-inducing boundaries possible, what does this say for the tendencies of his victim? After all, a narcissist has many victims and, thus, a multitude of boundaries that he can cross. The truth is that a narcissist is hardly interested in a woman with boundaries. *Come on, Zari, it can't be that simple!* Yup, it is. The main difference between a person who will tolerate narcissistic manipulation and a person who won't is a willingness to set boundaries. *In fact, setting personal boundaries (and then protecting them) is pretty much the **only** protection against narcissism for anyone.* A codependent is typically skittish about setting boundaries of *any* kind as this would indicate a willingness and ability to assume control over their own lives - and who has time for *that* with all this hoping going on?

Breaking this type of codependency is difficult because we associate the desperation that we feel with our love for the perpetrator. This causes mental confusion and an anxious willingness to hang in there.... to *try it one more time* because *maybe he'll change.* Our life becomes all about waiting for the narcissist's next move, hating the drama when we're in it, missing it when it's gone, and hoping, hoping, and more hoping. Then, before we know it, years have passed yet everything is exactly the same as it has always been.

In my opinion, this particular codependency (by my definition) is the saddest and most bittersweet of all the co-dependencies because it is based on two very positive human feelings/emotions: *love and hope*. Think about it...how we can't beat ourselves up for loving and hoping? With common types of co-dependencies, we can give things up – like drugs, booze, food, and even sex - and our chances of surviving happily are still good. But how do we commit ourselves to *giving up hope*? How do we reconcile the process that we need to *give up* on someone we love...*give up* on all hope...*give up* without ever looking back in order to be happy? For however long we've been involved, we've counted on this hope to get us through. How did our hope for a happy ending turn into a codependency that can never end happily? How are we *not* supposed to feel....deep down in our broken heart... that, maybe in some small way, hope failed *us*?

Below are a few of the signs and symptoms of the codependency you may feel to the narcissist in your life. On the surface, these "symptoms" may sound rather basic but the truth is that, when the controlling partner is a narcissist, the codependency is compounded. Keep in mind that passive-aggression, by its very nature, is often unspoken. Even if he won't cop to the intention, you just *know* what you're supposed to be doing. He will, in fact, gaslight you rather than ever admit that your suspicions are spot-on. *Baby, I don't know what you mean. Did you ever hear me* **say** *that? No. It's all in your mind. Stop acting crazy. It's freaking me out.* Things become so confusing and scary that you actually live day to day hoping that you're wrong about everything. Hope, hope, and more hope....

**For this exercise, I share a few of my own experiences with codependent "behavior" to use as examples. Tell me if I hit the nail on the head! Think about each example carefully and then, in the space that follows, share a story or simply talk about how this resonates with your current/past situation. Describe how you've felt or how this particular behavior does or doesn't remind you of** *you.* **We need to paint a clear picture for ourselves of our level of attachment before we can fully break it once and for all.**

**1.** In a codependent relationship, you will often find yourself *waiting* to do something or to interact with the narcissist. You become hesitant to make plans without him and may stop making plans altogether *unless* they include him. Consequently, you may find yourself often sitting around doing nothing because God knows the narcissist doesn't put *you* at the top of his list of activity partners. Basically, you allow your social life with anybody other than the narcissist to deliberately become non-existent.

*This happened to me all the time. It often seemed that my entire schedule was based on what he was or wasn't doing – and typically both of those things did not include me. I would cancel plans with friends or pass on the invitation or simply procrastinate long enough to where it became basically too late for me to show up. Invariably, I would end up sitting at home waiting for a phone call or for him to maybe pop in but that was still better than any repercussions I might receive for not being around when he called or came by.*

**How about you? Did you find yourself revolving your life around the narcissist's schedule and temperament?**

_____

_____

_____

_____

_____

_____

_____

_____

_____

_____

**2.** In conjunction with #1, you, as a codependent, will often find yourself doing things or not doing things based on the narcissist's passive-aggressive manner of enforcing ultimatums. He may clearly disapprove of certain friends and/or activities that you enjoy and, as retaliation, he may "threaten" you with certain friends and activities of his own. To avoid the emotional consequences, the codependent eventually finds it easier just to avoid doing anything or seeing anyone who may cause conflict in the relationship. When this happens, of course, we can safely assume that the narcissist's pathological relationship agenda is going according to schedule.

> *My ex would make comments under his breath every time a certain girlfriend called. He'd also become either completely silent if he thought I was going somewhere or he'd threaten me with a "read between the lines" scenario that would put a knot in my stomach. He'd smirk and say, "Sure, you do what you want. Really, I don't care. Well, I gotta get going...uh, you can try to call me later...". I knew then that if I did go out and try to call later, he wouldn't answer, thus elevating my fears that he was with someone else. And, as punishment for even considering the event, I also knew that he was probably going silent on me anyway. Either way, I was fucked. Eventually, I went nowhere and did nothing and even disconnected the home phone while he was over so my girlfriends wouldn't call me.*

**Relative to friends and activities, what was *your* situation like? How often did you feel that certain plans were thwarted due to your partner's direct or indirect threats toward the relationship? How did this make you feel and did it change the way you lived your life?**

_____

_____

_____

_____

_____

_____

_____

_____

_____

_____

_____

_____

_____

_____

_____

–

**3.** Your codependency, to the narcissist, deserves no breaks. In other words, there are never going to be moments that you will ever feel free. To cover his own ass, the N intentionally creates chaos so that you remain in a heightened state of anxiety 24/7. For you, this means feeling anxious and insecure even during non-threatening, mandatory day-to-day events such as work, school, dinner at your parent's, etc. Wherever you go, you are subjected to his emotional shenanigans via phone, text, and maybe even by random "pop-in". However he does it, the intention is that you always feel unable to relax in your own skin. Filled with anxiety, you find it difficult to 1) *smile* (let alone enjoy the moment), 2) concentrate or focus during important events, or 3) think of anything other that what he might be doing or who he might be doing it *with*. Often, you may even to choose to leave work early, feign sickness, cancel dinner with friends, or sneak out of class early just to drive to where he's at. His point, of course, is that you never forget who's in control, bitch!

**During day to day activities or when you *did* choose to get away alone or with friends, were you able to enjoy yourself freely or were there times that you remember being completely consumed by his passive-aggressive threats and behaviors?**

---
---
---
---
---
---
---
---
---
---
---

I believe that everything we do in this relationship is based on our incessant codependency to *hope*. We hope that things can change and that we'll discover we were wrong all along. The behaviors of a narcissist, again, are so unfathomable that it's hard to believe that *he really did that*. Our hope is all we have and we cling to it, going back and forth and allowing him to return again and again. But the truth, of course, is that narcissists, sociopaths, and psychopaths can *never be fixed* – not with love, not with therapy, and not with any pill under the sun. No matter who we are, no matter what we do, no matter how much love we give, no matter how hard we hope, hope, and hope.....nothing will *ever* make a difference in how this person behaves. *That* part is completely out of our hands. What we do with our own lives...the choices we make that allow ourselves to be treated this way...is up to us. In *this*, we have complete control.

# Exercise 3d:
## Creating Deal-Breakers

I said it before and I'll say it again, don't – *under any circumstances* - settle for crumbs in your life *anymore*. We can't continue to forfeit boundaries and deal-breakers that, in the end, would have saved our lives, saved us from the suffering and anxiety, saved us *from ourselves* and from that false, false love that we now have to recover from. Life is so very short and every moment far too precious to waste on loving a toxic, unfixable person. If narcissists are perfectly happy living their lives in disguise on the pretense of a lie, then let them be so they can do just that. Going forward, we simply can't afford to let ourselves falter on boundary protection.

Now, although they may appear similar, deal-breakers and boundaries are not one in the same. Whereas personal boundaries are basically unspoken and represent something *about ourselves* that we need to protect, a deal-breaker is something *about someone else* that we'd prefer to protect ourselves *from*. Deal-breakers, too, represent how we feel about things and may even represent a belief system but, overall, our creation of deal-breakers is based on our opinion only and more or less tells the world what we might be willing to or absolutely won't accept in the next person we sleep with, date, marry, or what have you.

Deal-breakers, if you create them appropriately, will help

you *weed out* the boundary crossers in one fell swoop. Keep in mind that even if a quality, habit, or characteristic about someone doesn't exactly float your boat, it's not necessarily a deal-breaker unless you say it is. And what may be a deal-breaker for you might actually be a turn-on for someone else. And just because a person has too many deal-breakers for your likening doesn't necessarily mean he or she is a bad person, it just means that the two of you may be better off as friends.

I think it's very important that, as part of the recovery plan, we get absolutely "right" with our boundaries and deal-breakers. Boundaries and deal-breakers are our only protection against the narcissists and other emotional manipulators that walk this planet. A boundary, of course, protects us at the deeper emotional level because the violation of a boundary can be so personal. To discover a deal-breaker in someone simply means that we have to make a choice. We can stop associating with this person or we can continue on, choosing instead to *compromise* based on the qualities that we *do* like about that person. We must decide whether the good qualities are *good enough* to override the deal-breakers and sometimes they are and sometimes they are *not*. The key, however, is to take our decision seriously because deal-breakers offer a world of insight and go a long way towards helping us weed out potential boundary crossers.

*From now on, I refuse to continue to keep company with anyone who.....*

*1. ..doesn't have my "back" all of the time – meaning in my defense, in times of crisis, and even when we are angry with each other for something unrelated.*

*2. ...behaves in a way that makes me feel even the slightest bit compelled to "investigative" or fact-check*

*3....subjects me to silent treatment for even five minutes (never mind five weeks!)*

*4...has difficulty assuming responsibility for even the simplest things*

*5...attempts to turn others (my friends, family, etc.) against me when it suits his purpose*

*6. ...treats me one way in bed and another way with his clothes on*

*7...is a continual promise-breaker*

*8...is disrespectful of my job, my property, and my personal possessions*

*9...goes for any length of time without a phone or changes his cell phone number for any reason whatsoever*

*10...cheats on me even one time*

*11...doesn't say what they mean and mean what they say*

*12...makes me doubt or question, even for a second, my gut feeling or my memory of an event.*

The list, of course, could go on and on. When I was writing the chapter on deal-breakers for *When Love Is a Lie*, I remember having great difficulty weeding down my initial list of 100 to the forty or so that finally made it to the book. It's amazing how looking back in retrospect can bring such clarity. How was it that I had no problem creating, just a few months after the break-up, a list of well over one-hundred deal-breakers yet for thirteen-years I never held the narcissist to a single one?

**How about you? Going forward, what are some of the deal-breakers that you can use to weed out the boundary crossers? What's important to you in a person? Think of your undeniable truths and the boundaries that you created in the earlier exercises and make a nice long list!**

_____

_____

_____

_____

_____

_____

_____

_____

_____

_____

_____

_____

_____

_____

_____

_____

_____

_____

_____

Transform your codependency to hope into something wonderful by allowing yourself to mentally break free from the grip of the narcissist. From this moment going forward, your life is going to change.

# Some Final Thoughts:
## No Contact & Being Single

I closed *When Love Is a Lie* with some final thoughts about No Contact (NC) and I find it appropriate to do the same here. While it might be hard now, once you've started working on your recovery, you will find "no contact" easier and easier to maintain. For this reason alone, I will continue to stress the importance of working towards recovery – whether it's by using this workbook or some other method – *even if you are still in the relationship.* There's no time like now to mentally break free.

If you are at the point of no contact, you must be clear about your intention and vigilant with your attack. Playing by the No Contact Rules means *just that* and there are many wonderful, fun ways to enforce it: blocking his number and email, not answering the door, de-friending and blocking from Facebook or deleting your own account temporarily, refraining from drunk text-messaging or letter-sending, swearing off drive-bys in the middle of the night, changing *your* cell number, moving across town or even to another state if necessary, changing jobs if the narcs is a co-worker, avoiding mutual friends and social circles, and so forth and so on. NC, of course, gets better and easier with time but I'm telling you right now that you can feel better *now* – even if you *are still with* this person.

Be aware of your own behaviors. Oftentimes when we go NC, we are actually using a reverse silent treatment to lure this person back into our lives. If this is the case, the narcissist *will* recognize your intention and continue to play right along, turning your life into an endless cycle of seduce-and-discard with each discard being more painful than the one before. If you remain focused and clear with your intention, you *will* be able to catch yourself before a fall. You will be able to pull your power back.

As I said in *When Love Is a Lie*, breaking no contact is not the end of the world; it's only the end of no contact. Cut yourself as much slack as possible as you climb out of the rabbit hole. Get up, dust yourself off, and start again if necessary. In many ways, our codependency to hope is an addiction just like any other....it's a compulsive way to self-medicate. The biggest difference is that self-medicating this way rarely feels good. It's hardly worth all the trouble we put ourselves through.

If you're not ready to go NC, then fall back on Silence Appreciation and use to its full advantage for as long as it lasts. Use the time productively...to breathe, to write in a journal, to write a book, to become angry rather than sad....to do all those things you can't do when he's manipulating the situation *and your life* to suit his own purpose. Your recovery will make you feel the whole spectrum of human emotions...but you must do it. And I *know* you can.

### *....and on being single*

Now, when I was younger, I truly believed that the best way to get over an ex was to find someone new right away and that's what I would do. And while, for many, many years, this method of relationship rehab actually worked, I know now that it only worked because the relationships that had just ended were, for all intents and purposes, *normal* relationships and therefore the pain was truly temporary and passed quickly as soon as I found someone I liked. During those times, I still remember missing that other person and feeling hurt by the break-up, but it was different. When a relationship break-up is "normal", life simply moves forward without a whole lot of effort. This is the way it's supposed to be whether you find someone else or not. *You're not supposed to shrivel up and die because a relationship ends or some asshole walks away.*

Now, that being said, when your partner in the ended relationship was a narcissist, the residual damage is much, much different as are the psychological tools that could possibly help us to recover. I certainly can't speak for everyone here - and it's possible I'm speaking for no one - but allow me to use myself as an example to explain why I honestly feel that jumping in the sack with the next best thing when you're trying to get over the narcissist is not really a great idea.

You see, just because the ex-narcissist/psychopath has already hooked his next victim doesn't mean that we have to jump on the same band wagon. The N/P does it because *that's what he does* and will always do. You need to think rationally when it comes to this part or else you'll find yourself back in the same sinking boat you just jumped out of. I, for one, didn't think rationally about this at all *many* times during periods that the narcissist and I were apart and I don't feel very proud of the memory.

Over those twelve years, there were certain splits initiated by the N during which sitting around and crying was not my first order of business. In fact, it never took long before some attractive, funny guy would step in to temporarily fill the void, providing me with a distraction that certainly should have lasted longer than twenty-four to forty-eight hours. But it never did although I'd always hope *going in* that it would (and there's that *hope* thing again). Nope, I never gave any of those guys a chance – not a single one of them – even while presenting myself as a very enthusiastic date. Inevitably, something this new person would do – some benign behavior - would inevitably make me suddenly and desperately miss the N. It was never a rational moment but when it occurred, *I was done*. Suddenly, I went from being a nice girl to a girl not much different than the N. I would - as shameful as it is - simply disappear. Without warning, I'd stop answering the phone or returning texts and this poor new guy – whoever it happened to be - would invariably get slightly panicked for a week or two and then, eventually, much to my relief, he would just fade away. In the back of my mind, having him fade away on those terms meant less of a chance that he'd resurface after the N and I got back together. And, after all, that *was* my conditioned intention all alone, of course – to get back together with the N - and we always did.

I wish I could say that each of the guys that I behaved this way with were jerks or inappropriate people in some way but I have to be honest and say that I remember very clearly that none of them were. I, on the other hand, acted like a jerk – just as if I were the N himself. And for that, I'm not very happy.

In retrospect, I'm smart enough to know that if I had waited a good period of time....time enough to think about the whole damn thing...time enough to have worked through the parts of the process with, say, a workbook of this nature...I might have given a one of those decent guys a fighting chance. Or, better yet, I would have avoided the whole hurtful situation and simply stayed single so I could get my shit together.

By jumping right into a situation where any little flaw...any little uncomfortable moment...made me suddenly miss the passive-aggressive dysfunction and abuse of my previous relationship, I was just priming myself to get back with the N as soon as he was ready. The fact that we even miss the narcissist at all has everything to do with how low they manage down our relationship expectations. We become convinced - in the back of our damaged minds - that we *miss* the measly crumbs of attention....that we *want* those measly crumbs. Because I wasn't ready emotionally, I was willing to kick a nice guy to the curb in order to get those crumbs back in my life! Staying present in the moment and working through the pain before I even *entertained* the thought of seeing another man would have avoided all of that.

Be good to yourself and be mindful of the present moment. Understand that any time spent with a narcissist is time wasted and *none of us have time to waste.* Watch for the signs, the red flags, and learn from the mistakes of others. Make the steps of your recovery a big part of every day. Separate from the sadness one day at a time. Fight the urge to succumb to the hovering and commit yourself to no contact at all costs. Memorize the boundaries and deal-breakers you've created in this workbook and guard them with your life. They are your only protection from someone who has a narcissistic personality. Don't dwell on the history of your relationship because it was a history based on a lie and you deserve better. Make a new history with a person who is worthy of your attention. Make your undeniable truths the foundation for what you believe and know in your heart to be true *from this moment forward.*

Return to this workbook whenever you need to and redo the exercises. Contact me via my website and let me know your story as well as the progress of your recovery. It's a learning experience for everyone - including myself – and I welcome the opportunity to hear from you.

Go forward, find your happiness, and have the beautiful life that you so deserve.

#####

## *Expect the Truth, Expect Recovery*

### *Speak w/ Zari*

**Affordable Consultations Available**

**Visit Zari's Blog: thenarcissisticpersonality.com**

# ABOUT THE AUTHOR

Zari Ballard is a home-based Freelance Writer/Author (and single mom!) who resides in sunny Tucson, Arizona at the base of the beautiful Catalina Mountains. In 2005, four years after her son's diagnosis with child-onset schizophrenia, Zari set aside the corporate rat race in lieu of a home-based career as a Freelance Writer. A leap of faith that could have gone either way, the choice was meant-to-be and she has never looked back.

Now, along with providing ghostwriting services to a handful of long-time clients, Zari plans to dive head first into self-publishing for the second half of 2013. Readers will soon enjoy two new additions to Zari's Amazon Bookshelf (alongside *When Love Is a Lie*) - a memoir about her son's life as well as a fictional Kindle novel about the end times. Be sure and stay tuned!

P.S. Zari's been narcissist-free since 10/2012 and plans to keep it that way....:)

Visit my blog **TheNarcissistPersonality.com**

# BONUS SECTION:
## Special Book Excerpt


# *When Love Is a Lie*

### Narcissistic Partners & the Pathological Relationship Agenda

*Zari Ballard*

# Chapter I
## *Something Wicked*

*They lie even when the truth is a better story.* Now, I don't know exactly where I read that line - or if it even referred to narcissism - but I never forgot it. To me, it so perfectly describes the wickedness of the narcissistic mentality....the chilling way that *everything* about *anything* a narcissist says or does is based on a lie. Whether a narcissist lies by making things up or by leaving things out is inconsequential because he (or she) is *always* up to no good and keeping secrets is a priority. Oh yes, and there are *always* secrets...so many, in fact, that a narcissist will tell a lie even if the truth is a better story...even if the truth would keep him out of trouble or dissuade our suspicions. Some believe this happens because the narcissist actually believes the lie but I disagree. I think that a narcissist lies all the time because it's an easy way to emotionally devastate the recipient and because lying allows the narcissist/sociopath to recreate himself on the fly, thus creating an environment where he can always be giving himself props for *getting away* with something. After all, to a narcissist, lies - just like emotions - are a means to an end as well.

It is the outright wickedness of the pathological narcissist that is truly mind-boggling and if I thought, by writing this book, that I could cathartically cleanse myself of the bafflement, I was only partly right. Accepting the fact that everything that *appeared* to be true in a relationship was, in fact, a complete and utter fabrication, a figment of our imagination, and a *waste of precious time that we can never get recoup* is a hard pill to swallow. Our love, in fact, was a lie.

In my relationship, the length of time from the N's return after a silent treatment to the point where he would, once again, begin ramping up the chaos in preparation to go silent again gradually grew shorter and shorter. To my ex, the periodic moments of normalcy/calmness in our relationship would instantly trigger warning bells in his twisted head. *Uh-oh, I think we're getting along here. Fuck that. I'll show her!* I came to understand that any time we shared having great sex and camaraderie did not come without a price. Inevitably, at the tail-end of a calm afternoon or evening - and only after he was certain I'd dropped my guard and completely relaxed - he'd find some insane way to cripple me on his way out. For me, just the *anticipation* of the axe falling would cause me tremendous anxiety. It became impossible for me to relish in the moment and I let him know it. "How can I relax when I *know* what's going to happen here....when I can predict your next move?" I'd ask him, hoping for a sign...a comforting word...that this time, perhaps, would be different. It never happened. Instead, his response, true to form, was always to *gaslight* me...to minimize the truth of my words...to make me believe I was losing my mind. "Why do you have to be so fucking negative?" he'd say. "All you do is bring up the past. You're delusional and I'm getting tired of all of it." And then, of course, he'd proceed to prove me right anyway *every time*. Days later, when I'd try to talk about it, calmly laying out the facts and trying logically to convince him that it was his repeated behaviors that enabled my ability to predict, he'd look at me like he didn't have the slightest idea *what* I was talking about.

So, to me, it only stands to reason that the behaviors of the manipulative, pathological, and passive-aggressive narcissist would continue to drive us batty, throwing us into crazy, repetitive "ground-hog day" cycles of digging and searching and analyzing and ruminating - over and over and over - for answers that simply aren't there. Our reactions to these human anomalies are *natural*. The fact is that even the most unremarkable, commonplace narcissist will continue to lie and abuse *because it's simply what he does*. Amazingly, I've come to realize that there doesn't have to be a damn thing special about these guys to make them what they are. Intellects, occupations, nationalities, and ages may vary across the board but the behaviors *worldwide* are exactly the same. So, what normal human being *wouldn't* go nuts trying to figure it all out? Whether this realization makes the reality any easier to bear, I'm not so sure…but it is what it is.

What I can tell you, however, is that over time, by making a conscious effort to change my thought process, I felt things starting to shift in my favor. Now, I never knew exactly how (or even when) things would shift but I would, every once in a while, just know that they *had* because certain frenetic behaviors of mine would simply stop. For example, for a good part of twelve years, whenever subjected to a silent treatment or unexpected dismissal by the narcissist, I would feel compelled to take to the streets in the wee hours of the morning, five-page letter in hand and butterflies in my stomach, hoping to either catch him in the act of *something* or at least connect (albeit by proxy...the letter). Over the years, I must have written nearly a thousand letters to the N – all heart-felt pleas for peace, begging him, in desperation, to change his ways, end the silent treatment, and come back to the fold. Sometimes this tactic worked, sometimes it didn't, but the writing and re-writing, always trying to get the words *just right*, exhausted me every time. *Then* would come the drive across town and the nerve-wracking moments of tip-toeing to the apartment door to attach the letter, my heart pounding out of my chest. Sometimes he'd be home, sometimes he'd be out, but it mattered not because the anxiety was the same. Minutes later, as I made my way home, then and only then, did I feel the huge wave of relief that made it all worthwhile....the feeling that I'd *connected* and that perhaps he'd respond and the silence would end. Up *until* that point, I'd feel absolutely *consumed.*

In retrospect, of course, I see that my behaviors were crazy-making. Fueled by narcissistic manipulation, these late night rituals of writing and driving became my defining purpose in the relationship. *His* defining purpose was to create the chaos that he knew compelled me to behave that way. And around and around it went. The crazier he could make me, the better he felt about us, about himself, and about his entire existence. All I ever felt was crazy.

Then, one night, on my way out the door with letter and keys in hand, I felt a sudden and unexpected shifting in my mindset....kind of like an earthquake shaking loose the petrified pieces of my common sense. For the first time in years, I looked at the clock, thought about how tired I felt, how late I'd get back, and about all of the anxiety-filled miles between my front door and his....and simply didn't go. My heart-heavy weariness and my common sense *finally became bigger* than the urge to chase the N and participate in the game. I knew, in that split second, that my nightly ritual of driving across town in the middle of the night during a silent treatment was over...that at least my participation in *that* part of the manipulation game had ended. *My God, what would I do with all my free time? Sleep, maybe?* Somehow, by the grace of God, I had been granted a semblance of control within the chaos and I relaxed that night for the first time in years.

Normally a fairly sensible person, I had begun to feel, as the years passed, a slipping away of my own ability to respond appropriately to the N's hurtful behaviors. It was as if my abilities to either stand up for myself or to detach when necessary were being very methodically "conditioned away" by the N himself. Questionable as that may sound to some, those of you who've experienced this type of manipulation will know *exactly* what I'm talking about. It was the N's *intention* for me to leave endless voice mails and to cry and write letters and drive around at all hours when he disappeared. If, at any given time, he was feeling *particularly* evil or planned to be with another source of narcissistic supply for longer than a week, he would even opt to change his cell number, ramping up my insanity even further. He changed his cell number so many times during one three-year stretch that I became confused as to which number he *did* have when we were back together. Eventually, just like the urge to write and drive, the urge I always felt to call him, leaving voice mail after frantic voice mail, demanding answers or begging him to snap out of it disappeared as well with that mysterious mental shift. And, again, it was an amazing relief.

Throughout all of the madness, the N became very adept at strategically controlling any given situation. Cleverly passive-aggressive, his behaviors made me doubt my confidence and my own stability and, thus, ensured both of his own. To be clear, a narcissist doesn't typically sit down with a pen and paper and write out his narcissistic plan step by step. He just *does* it, learning himself, over time, what works and what doesn't and just how far he can push the envelope. So when, little by little, I'd stop participating in parts the game, he'd instinctively know something was up and invariably end his silence early, pressing down on the proverbial relationship reset button (that only narcissists have, by the way) and reappearing at my doorstep without a logical explanation in sight. And I always took him back. I was determined, in my own mind, to see it through…to figure out, once and for all, if the dysfunction in our relationship was, in fact, *my* doing (as he adamantly wanted me to believe). If that were true, and it was my behavior that made him suddenly disappear, then the rattling loose of my common sense and my new disinterest in N-stalking rituals would certainly change things, right? Surely, if I just let things be, everything would calm down and perhaps get back to "normal". Hell, I was all for *that.* I mean, he couldn't possibly *want* the chaos, could he?

Then, one day, as I was driving him into town, the N made a comment that gave me my first profound "a-ha" moment in the relationship. This happened during a particularly secretive time where even his place of residence was a mystery so, to the N, my new non-confrontational demeanor was highly unusual and maybe even suspicious. Somewhere during the one-sided conversation on the drive in, he suddenly defiantly announced that it was obvious *I didn't love him the same way that I used to* and that he was fairly certain *I wouldn't love him like that again.* At that moment, I was completely confused. What did he mean, *like that?* Like *what?* I was missing his point and I said so. Frustrated, he waited until we came to a red light and then he simply opened the door and got out, leaving me sitting there dumbfounded. But I didn't go after him. Instead, I flipped a u-turn and headed back home quietly pissed. He thought I didn't *love him? Me? Didn't he see how hard I was trying?* Halfway there, it suddenly occurred to me that, to Wayne, it was all about the behaviors *I didn't do anymore* that indicated to him my lack of love. Son-of-a-bitch! As if a floodlight had kicked on, I immediately understood. He *wanted* me to love him *like that* – to be crazy and jealous and out of my fucking mind. He *liked it* like that. Without the chaos, he simply wasn't that interested. The more I suffered, *the more he knew I really cared!* It was my first "a-ha" moment in the relationship and it propelled me to shift even faster.

As you read through the coming chapters, I hope that, at the very least, you will feel a *shift*....a change in your vision....a nudge in the right direction. You'll "get it" because you're smart and beautiful and you are here searching for help and for answers. I know how it is and everything about this type of relationship is complicated – from the manipulation to the methods of his control to your feelings about him, yourself, and your life....nothing about it is an easy resolve. For me, I had so much time and emotion invested in the mess that, even as horrid as it was, I didn't *want* to give up. I know now, of course, that ending the torment *years* earlier (or at least after making my discovery) would have salvaged a good part of my forties. But I just couldn't do it. I *wanted* to love him unconditionally no matter what dark secrets he had. I wanted to find out the truth and I then I wanted to fix it. So, I stayed. And after I found out the truth, I *still* stayed, hoping that somehow he'd prove me wrong.

If you're reading this book on the brink of discovery...well, brace for impact because the information and personal experiences

I share here will confirm your suspicions. Since I'm neither a doctor nor a psychologist (and I don't pretend to be), I can only describe for you my experiences and all that I have learned. I understand full well that a relationship involving a narcissistic partner is very, very different than even the most dysfunctional of "normal" relationships. Because of those differences, outsiders looking in on your situation are never going to understand the level of betrayal. People assume you lay all the blame on the narcissist and take no accountability for your own behaviors and this simply isn't true. In fact, most of us started blaming ourselves long before we even started to question the narcissist. Accountability is actually part of the reason we stay. The last thing that we'd ever want to become in our relationship is a quitter! But the fact is that there are going to be people – and even those who are close to us – that believe that quitting is the only thing we should be doing. Oh if it were only that easy!

For me, it's become quite easy to pinpoint those readers who haven't actually experienced an involvement with a narcissist but are reading my books for reasons unrelated. Invariably, they will leave reviews or comments stating that I'm nothing more than a bitter girlfriend or that I pander to whiners and that anyone who stays in a relationship such as I describe needs professional help. Even if they keep their thoughts to themselves, we have to assume that this will be typical of what others are thinking and we have to accept it. How can we possibly expect others to understand what we're going through if we barely understand it ourselves? It's too complex a situation.

But oh boy, when we *do* "get it"…when, in that split second of the "aha" moment, everything clicks and the dots connect…when the *what, why, and how* of the narcissist's agenda comes together in a millisecond….it takes our very breath away and the ground beneath our feet never again feels quite secure. If you haven't had the "aha" moment yet, this book could very be the trigger-pull that makes it happen. If, by chance, I happen to enlighten and/or empower even one reader to make the right decision, I will have more than exceeded my goal for this little book.

So, let us begin…

# Chapter II:
## *The Relationship Agenda*

Women (and men) who love narcissists are resilient, multi-tasking individuals. Not only are we babysitters for these motherfuckers, we are usually mothers or fathers, sisters or brothers, daughters or sons, breadwinners, students, homeowners, business owners, professionals, and more at the same time. Like everyone else in the world, our entire existence is about doing whatever we can to survive and, for the most part, we're damn good at it. This is fairly amazing since loving a narcissist is ridiculously time-consuming and obsessive....a feat above and beyond the normal expectations in most types of relationships.

What the N does is deliberately manipulate every possible situation so that he fully dominates our thought process. This, in and of itself, is the most debilitating part of what I have deemed the narcissist's **pathological relationship agenda**. It's incredibly difficult to live our lives when half of our brain is focused on this one individual. We can never quite relax in our own mind because the N is always conjuring up new ways to keep us unbalanced and insecure. This is not only part of his plan, it is the key objective of the relationship agenda...and the narcissist, too, is very good at what *he* does.

The narcissist's relationship agenda is his modus operandi

169

for living. He has no other choice but to satisfy the agenda to the best of his ability or life, as he knows it, would be far from worth living. Now, the nature of this agenda being part of a personality "disorder" does not make it okay, it just makes it what it is. We don't have to accept it or adhere to it or allow the narcissist's determination to fulfill it get in the way of our lives. The fact that we do is my biggest reason for sharing with you the process that mentally set me free.

When it comes to leaving an N, nobody *gets it* that we already *know* what our options are. We can walk away, run away, slam the door, quit the job, stop answering the phone, delete the texts, block his emails….we *know* all that. And most of us even *do* all that. But leaving an N, going No Contact….it's a break-up, clearly, but nothing really severs. For a long time after, if we dare to look over our shoulder, there'll be the narcissist, sticking out his evil fork-shaped tongue, like a lizard to a fly, waiting to eat us alive once again. There's a reason why some victims of this type of abuse *never* fully recover once they *do* break free.

After discovering the meaning of narcissism, I couldn't get enough information on the subject. I was simultaneously sickened and fascinated by the way that everything I read on the topic appeared to have been written for *me*. I looked for excuses to hang on (there were none) and reasons to leave (there were zillions) but one thing was very clear to me throughout and couldn't be denied any longer - a narcissist/sociopath can ***never be fixed* – not with**

**love, not with therapy, and not with any pill under the sun.** The relationship will never get better because the N *likes it just the way it is.* His plan, his relationship agenda from day one (which is always clear in his mind) is to keep you, as his main yet secondary source of supply, in a perpetual state of heightened anxiety. Yes, that's right...you, as his *main* squeeze, is actually *secondary* in his life to his multiple *primary* sources – that being all of the additional women, men, and extracurricular dalliances he has on the side. Sadly, you are not the most important relationship in his life but rather the relationship that is the *most convenient* because the effort to keep you in the game is so minimal. With all systems in place, the N happily gets what he wants from life which is a big piece of sugary cake and all the time in the world to eat it. Don't ever forget that when you suffer, he wins. Why? Because, according to the narcissist's relationship agenda, *your suffering is the narcissist's reward for a job well done.*

*Every* narcissist has a relationship agenda and, for the most part, it's *always* pathological – hence, my rather simplistic creation of the term *pathological relationship agenda* which I use to describe (and explain) the **universal** behaviors of narcissists and sociopaths in relationship situations. The rules and requirements of this agenda rarely ever change and, thus, will always dictate to a narcissist the appropriate narcissistic behaviors for any given situation. In my imagination (which, I admit, can be twisted), I envision that baby narcissists spiritually inherit the actual agenda playbook probably *before* birth and that this playbook

171

automatically updates *universally* as these narcissists get older. I also imagine the adult narcissist thumbing through the pages of this playbook on a daily basis, memorizing and devouring the specifics of the agenda's relationship requirements. It's as if each N is predisposed to want to be the best narcissist *ever*....to get the most bang in life (at the expense of others) for his narcissistic buck. Moreover, it appears that success is guaranteed because, honestly, I've never heard of a narcissist who *failed* at being a narcissist. If a narcissist fails, it's because he's not a narcissist.

Whether a narcissist really has a choice in the matter of becoming a narcissist is an entirely different topic for another book at another time. The important thing now is that you understand that, as victims of narcissism, we basically live the same life. By this, I mean that my narcissist is like your narcissist is like her narcissist is like his narcissist. The agenda ideology that empowers a narcissist to live his life in the manner that he does is akin to his/her "religion" and it is, without a doubt, universal. A narcissist, male or female, will basically do the same things, exhibit the same behaviors, say the same words, inflict the same passive-aggressive pain, and follow the same narcissistic patterns all the time, *every* time. If you think I'm exaggerating, I urge you to keep reading. By the third chapter of this book, you'll find yourself wondering if maybe *my* boyfriend was *your* boyfriend. By the end of the book, you'll be *convinced* of it.

Now, to be fair, we have to consider that the astounding

similarities between all of our partners certainly can be attributed to clinical factors. According to most medical/psychology books, narcissism is invariably defined as a personality disorder that forms in early childhood from some type of abuse and/or neglect within a parent/child relationship where at least one parent (usually the mother) is a narcissist or sociopath. I believe that most of us have figured this out and, granted, this definition *does* fit most commonplace narcissists to a tee, my ex included. However, what good does knowing this information ever do to alleviate the problem? When backed into a corner, my ex would predictably use the "abused childhood" excuse to the point that, over time, I went from being ridiculously sympathetic to screaming "Get over it!" (and you can surely guess how that worked out for me!). Even now, although I did witness the love/hate between him and his mom, I'm not absolutely convinced that the dynamic of the abuse was even true. It's very possible that an online article clued him in to the excuse – who knows? The N's lack of sincerity about *anything* makes it impossible for us to distinguish between fact and fiction. We can only rely on our gut instincts because this, at least, will never fail us.

The bottom line is that a narcissist is a bad seed, an empty human shell void and incapable of feelings, empathy, conscience and love…an entity that I dare say might be one of God's few but biggest mistakes – *and one that certainly can't be fixed.* With nearly three million predatory male and female narcissists walking the earth, this is truly a scary time for anyone seeking a partner in life. Moreover, since a narcissist's very survival is guaranteed *only* by fulfilling his relationship agenda, he/she will always be seeking out and sucking in an endless influx of **narcissistic supply.** As the partner, you have to understand that the cycle of manipulation will continue until the day he dies or until you die, whichever comes first. This is why, no matter what you do or say or how much you love this person, the situation never gets any better. It simply can't and it never will.

So, with all due respect to medical truisms, the self-serving definition of narcissism as a helpless disorder has no place on these pages. A narcissist partner, however "helpless", is still the enemy and so I've chosen to take a darkly humorous perspective of the individual which I feel is far more deserving. For example, when my son was younger, he and my ex were both very enthusiastic about the movie *The Terminator* (1984) starring Arnold Schwarzenegger (incidentally, one of the biggest narcissists of all time) and therefore we'd all seen it many times. One scene, in particular, always gave me pause because it seemed to describe precisely the mindset of the N. In this scene, the character Kyle (who has come from the past to save the heroine, Sara Conner, from her future demise) is trying desperately to convince Sara that the emotionless killing machine (Arnold) has a rock-solid agenda against her: *You still don't get it, do you? He'll find you! That's* ***what he does!*** *That's ALL he does! You can't stop him! He'll wade through you, reach down your throat, and pull your fuckin' heart out! He can't be bargained with. He can't be reasoned with. He* *doesn't feel pity, or remorse, or fear. And he absolutely will not stop, ever, until you are dead!"* Well, that about sums it up.

I understand that *you suspect something* about your relationship. You have a feeling that *something* – even if you can't quite put your finger on it – is very, very wrong. And you're right. The narcissist has a relationship agenda. To fulfill the relationship agenda, a narcissist will stop at nothing. He will cross all boundaries, stomp on your soul, and basically pull the trigger on the normalcy of life until *you* end it. And it is *you* who must end the madness because the narcissist never will.

*Let there be no mistake how the enemy will be painted on the coming pages.*

# Chapter III:

## *Recognize the Basic Signs*

If you suspect that you may be a victim of narcissistic manipulation in your relationship, the behavioral signs listed in this chapter will most likely confirm your fears. As you read through the list, look deep into the descriptions, replaying in your mind the matching behaviors of your partner - the ones that made you scratch your head, question your intuition, question your *sanity* (and *his*), apologize for nothing, scream like a banshee, or say nothing at all to avoid the confrontation. *Those* behaviors.

What complicates the recognition of narcissistic manipulation in a relationship is that the signs, particularly during the first year of a relationship, are deliberately subtle…deliberately passive-aggressive. The unavailable man, psychopath, sociopath, narcissist – again, whatever you want to call him – is a very passive-aggressive individual with the patience of a saint when it comes to controlling others. This is exactly the reason why women don't often figure it all out until well past the point of no return. I was seven years in before I started even *looking* for answers or, for that matter, even knew there might be answers to look for. When my girlfriend Barbie, observing my anguish during the sixth week of yet *another* silent treatment, said "Well, he's obviously got all the time in world to make you suffer", I had my second "a-ha" moment of the relationship and it almost knocked me off my chair.

The list of "behaviors" that follows is the best *basic* list I've found of the emotionally manipulative tactics used by the narcissist abuser. As you read through each description, keep in mind that the N is a Master Manipulator for a reason: *subtlety is his strong point.*

So, are you ready? Let's see how well we resonate with the following list of narcissistic behaviors, attitudes, and relationship expectations:

### *13 Behaviors of a Narcissistic Partner:*

1. The N demands that you tolerate and cater to his every need and always be available when it works for him. He, of course, never has to be available for you - ever. Moreover, if you dare to even *question* his unavailability or show a "negative" emotion towards a manipulative behavior, you will quickly experience a narcissistic punishment such as a silent treatment (a narcissistic favorite) or a cold shoulder (if you live together) as a reminder of who has control.

2. The N is aware that he's aloof and indifferent and he knows this hurts you. By acting in this manner most of the time (and for no reason), a Narcissist is able to continually test the mental limits of your patience. The partner of a narcissist is always made to feel that something is slightly "off". You find yourself feeling compelled - and eventually obsessed - with finding answers to the unsettling experience of day to day life with a narcissist.

3. The N will jump at the chance to be physically abusive if you allow it because he or she always feels you deserve it. However, because physical abuse – as the narcissist knows – is far too obvious a slip of the narcissistic mask, the N will typically rely on his venomous mouth as the most effective means of inflicting emotional abuse and controlling you.

4. The N will cheat on you numerous times – of that you can be sure. If you catch him, he will dismiss your feelings, threaten to do it again to shut you up, or act as if you are making a big deal out of nothing. At the same time, he will accuse you of doing the very same thing. This is a distraction maneuver and one of the most hurtful ploys of a narcissist. *However,* because Ns are like children who give themselves away without knowing it, understand that whatever the N is accusing you of is *exactly* what he's up to at that moment in his life. **Turn his ploy into your advantage**.

5. Because a narcissist knows he is emotionally incapable of providing support, sympathy, or empathy, he will use his indifference to your life as a way to keep you unbalanced and confused as to his intentions. *For example, the N appears to be incapable of making plans with you and keeping them.* If you question this, he will act as if he hasn't a clue to what you are talking about. The truth, of course, is that to follow through with future plans involves pleasing another person and, therefore, he wants no part of it.

6. Over time, a narcissist slowly **manages down your expectations** of the relationship by putting forth only the most minimal *efforts* required to maintain his part (See Chapter VII). The N's main motto is **"just enough, just in time"** to keep the farce moving forward and not a bit more. Think about this and

you will see how true it is. To *deliberately* expend more effort than needed would indicate some level of predictability and well-intention on his part and just may "up" your expectations of him. Consequently, it will never happen and you will be punished in some way for pushing it. The N has no intention of filling anyone's expectation but his own.

7. The N is very good, when he needs to be, at *mimicking* the appropriate emotions of normal people to get a desired result or something that he needs. This is how he snagged you to being with and how he is able to attract women to him whenever he needs narcissistic supply. This is also how he is able to make you think all is okay right before a Discard so that his vanishing act confuses and hurts you the most.

8. The N truly believes that his presence is clearly and abundantly sufficient to maintain the loyalty, trust, affection, and respect that he expects from you (his object). Therefore, the narcissist will postpone, withhold, or procrastinate on any continuing, normal efforts that are essential to maintaining any kind of meaningful relationship. Again, this is another way the N manages down our expectations, allowing him to get away with more and more abuse.

**I hope you enjoyed this excerpt from *When Love Is a Lie.* The full version is available on Amazon Kindle and also in print from Amazon.com and selected retailers.**

Made in the USA
San Bernardino, CA
06 April 2018